Between Israel and Death

Between Israel and Death

Edward Bernard Glick

Stackpole Books

Published by
STACKPOLE BOOKS
Cameron and Kelker Streets
Harrisburg, Pa. 17105

Library of Congress Cataloging in Publication Data

Glick, Edward Bernard.
    Between Israel and death.

    Bibliography: p.
    1. Militarism—Israel. 2. Israel—Politics and government. 3. Israel.
Tseva haganah le-Yisrael.
I. Title.
DS126.5.G55   301.5'93'095694   74-506
ISBN 0-8117-0230-8

TO THE LATE
BENJAMIN MARCUS
and
CHARLES J. KATZ

Also by Edward Bernard Glick
Latin America and the Palestine Problem
Straddling the Isthmus of Tehuantepec
Peaceful Conflict
Soldiers, Scholars, and Society

Contents

Acknowledgments

ONE OF THE nicer chores of bookwriting is to acknowledge one's debt to the many people who help a writer to think, to write, and to see his words in print. It's a chore I perform gladly, but there's one thing wrong with it.

Tradition seems to demand that those of us who are both male and married acknowledge our wives last. I think it ought to be the other way around. True, my wife, Florence Wolfson Glick, won't type for me anymore—liberated female that she is. But with her critical eye and her critical ear she read and listened to every word in this book. She thus saved me from many a conceptual and stylistic idiocy. For this I am deeply grateful, as I am to Gail Cotton, my very capable research assistant at Temple University.

I also appreciate the kindness of the directors of PORI Public Opinion Research of Israel, Ltd., for permission to publish some of their surveys and of the following publishers for granting permission to quote and reprint portions from their magazines or books: *The Columbia Journal of World Business, Israel Magazine, Jewish Frontier,* The University of Chicago Press, publishers of Sol Tax's *The Draft;* Hadar Publishing House, Ltd., publishers of Moshe Ben-Shaul's *Generals of Israel;* The Israel Government's Central Bureau of Statistics, publishers of *Statistical Abstract of Israel;* Praeger Publishers, Inc., publishers of J. C. Hurewitz's *Middle East Politics: The Military Dimension;* and Weidenfeld and Nicolson, publishers of Shabtai Teveth's *The Cursed Blessing* and *Moshe Dayan.*

Since this book deals with Israel and her army—which has fought four major wars with the Arabs in twenty-five years—the first group of people I must thank are those Israelis who gave me some of their precious time. (What is more precious in life than time?) They are (with the ranks and/or jobs they held when I last interviewed them): Labor Minister Yosef Almogi, Lieutenant Colonel Eli Bar-Lev of the Army's Public Relations Branch, Colonel Mordechai M. Bar-On, Chief Education Officer of the Army; Colonel (Ret.) Israel Barnea of the Technological Museum of the Haifa Technion; Yitzchak Ben-Aharon, Secretary-General of the Histadrut, the giant Israeli labor union; Colonel Yosef Caleff, the Army Spokesman; Brigadier General Yerachmiel Dori, Chief Engineering Officer of the Army; Foreign Minister Abba Eban, the late Prime Minister Levi Eshkol, Zvi Gabay, Cultural Attaché of the Israeli Consulate-General in Philadelphia; Colonel (Ret.) Benjamin Gibli, Managing Director of the Shemen Company; Moshe Gilboa, Advisor to the Minister of Communications and of Transport; Rafael E. Gill, Director of PORI, Public Opinion Research of Israel, Ltd.; Major General (Ret.) Yehoshafat Harkabi, now a faculty member of The Hebrew University of Jerusalem; Avraham Harman, President of The Hebrew University; Colonel Baruch Levy, Commandant of the Military Boarding School near Tel-Aviv; Dr. Moshe Lissak, military sociologist at The Hebrew University; Dr. Yitzchak E. Nebenzahl, the State Comptroller; Colonel (Ret.) Moshe Netzer, Director of the Youth and Nahal Department of the Defense Ministry; Shimon Peres, who is both Minister of Transport and Minister of Communications; the late Arye Pincus, Chairman of the Jewish Agency and of the World Zionist Organization; Uri Radai, Secretary of the Defense and Foreign Affairs Committee of the Knesset, Israel's Parliament; Lieutenant General (Ret.) Yitzchak Rabin, Israeli Ambassador in Washington; Colonel Ram Ron, Israeli Military Attaché in Washington; Brigadier General Rafael Vardi, Military Governor of Judea and Samaria (the West Bank of occupied Jordan); Dr. Shevach Weiss of Haifa University, Dr. Simcha Werner of Bar-Ilan University, Eliezer Whartman, the Mutual Broadcasting System's Bureau Chief in Israel and my former neighbor in Jerusalem; Shalom Wurm, a member of Kibbutz Ramat Yochanan; Haim J. Zadok, the Chairman of the Knesset's Defense and Foreign Affairs Committee; Major General Eliahu Ze'ira, Chief of Military Intelligence; Lieutenant Colonel Yitzchak Ziv, Commandant of the Army's Marcus School in Haifa; and Colonel Musar Zohar, Commander of Gadna, the paramilitary youth corps, jointly administered by the Ministry of Defense and the Ministry of Education and Culture.

There were of course other Israelis, in and out of the Army or the government, who asked for and are receiving anonymity.

As for people in the United States, my thanks go to the members of the Committee on Research and Study Leaves of Temple University for grants as well as a sabbatical, which I spent in 1971 as a visiting professor at The Hebrew University. I am also very grateful to Dr. George W. Johnson, Dean of Temple's College of Liberal Arts, to Dr. Harold Lasswell, visiting professor of history, political science, and law at Temple, and to my good colleagues in our Department of Political Science—Profs. Harry A. Bailey, Jr. and Murray S. Stedman, Jr.

If my wife didn't do the typing or the endless little secretarial and clerical errands connected with "putting a book to bed," who did? Carol Grayson typed the final manuscript. Marnina Glick, Richard Jay Goldstein, Esther Pusey, Cynthia Reid, Linda Scherr, Monica R. Schisler, Zinna Schnee, and Doris Shinn all helped immeasurably in accomplishing the other tasks.

ACKNOWLEDGMENTS

Since I don't own a publishing house, I am terribly indebted to Stackpole Books, particularly Clyde P. Peters, the Executive Vice President; Phyllis C. Blocki, the Promotion Director; and Edward Walsh, my copyeditor. It has been a personal and professional pleasure to work with all three of them.

Lastly, I acknowledge my debt to my students: I could no more teach without writing than I could write without teaching.

Edward Bernard Glick

Between us and death stands only
Zahal. Zahal alone.
—Moshe Shamir on the eve of
the Six Day War

1

From the
Haganah to Zahal

EVEN A MODEST-SIZED general library contains a good number of books and articles by Israelis, Arabs, foreigners, scholars, journalists, politicians, and others on Zahal, the modern Israeli Army. If the library is larger or specialized, it contains, as well, the usual collections of official yearbooks and records, statistical abstracts, annual reports, brochures, pamphlets, and press releases—all with the usual variations in information, impartiality, insight, and interest.

Why, then, still another book on the Israeli Army? Because of at least three reasons. Previous books have either been written by scholars for scholars in the cold and colorless code-language of scholarship. Or they have stressed only one or two isolated aspects, such as history, politics, economics, or biography. Or they have related—sometimes in most exciting terms—how the Army of Israel is organized and how it fights and wins its wars and campaigns.

My purpose is something altogether different. It is to tell

the story of the two-way interaction between the people of Israel and the Army of Israel, particularly the latter's pervasive impact on *all* sectors of Israeli society. Perhaps I shall even succeed in explaining how Israel has so far managed to be a militarized but not militaristic, a disciplined but still democratic, modern garrison state.

The permeating influence of Zahal in Israeli society can perhaps be better understood when one realizes that its origin predates the founding of the state of Israel. The predecessor of the modern Israeli Army was the Haganah, the underground self-defense organization of the Jewish community during the period from 1918 to 1948 when the British ruled Palestine. In those years membership in the Haganah was wide but voluntary. And those who successfully passed its probationary period took the following oath:

> I hereby declare that, freely and voluntarily, I join the Hebrew Defense Organization in the land of Israel.
>
> I hereby swear that I shall remain faithful all the days of my life to the Defense Organization, to its code of law and its orders as defined in its Foundations by its High Command.
>
> I hereby swear that I am at the service of the Defense Organization all the days of my life, that I accept its discipline unconditionally and unreservedly, that I will obey its call to active duty anywhere and at any time, and that I will submit to all its commands and fulfill all its instructions.
>
> I hereby swear that I will dedicate all my strength, and if necessary give my life, for the defense of my people and my homeland, for the freedom of Israel and the redemption of Zion.

On May 31, 1948, when the new state was still being invaded by its neighbors, David Ben-Gurion, the country's first Prime Minister and Defense Minister—who in the most literal sense possible is Israel's George Washington—issued a famous and historic Order of the Day in "Year One of the Independence of Israel." It began: "With the establishment of the State of Israel the Haganah has left the underground to become a regular army." It continued: "Now a new chapter has opened. The regular army of the State of Israel, the army of Israel's freedom and independence in its own country, has been established . . . by the Provisional Government." And it included the following declaration:

Every male and female soldier serving in the army will swear the following oath:

"I swear and undertake, on my word of honor, to remain faithful to the State of Israel, to its laws and to its legally constituted authorities, to accept without reservation the discipline of the Israel Defense Forces, to obey all orders and instructions given by its authorized commanders, and to dedicate all my strength and even to sacrifice my life in the defense of the homeland and the freedom of Israel."

What was voluntary in the days of the Haganah has become compulsory in the days of Zahal, which is the Hebrew acronym and nickname for the Israel Defense Forces. This explains why one late Spring day in 1971, the year I lived in Jerusalem, regular readers of the *Jerusalem Post*, Israel's English-language daily, read this notice as they drank their morning tea or coffee and ate the delicious little Israeli rolls called *lachmaniyot:*

Defense Service Law 5719-1959
Male Israel citizens or permanent residents, who were born between September 9, 1926 and September 9, 1953, and who immigrated to Israel between October 1, 1949 and April 30, 1971, and who . . . have not yet received their Order to Report for Registration and Examination to determine their fitness for military service, must report at the recruiting office nearest their place of residence on June 9, 1971, at 8:00 A.M.
Those reporting . . . should bring with them their identity card, or the registration form issued by the Ministry of the Interior, or their birth certificate, together with their immigrant card and passport.

Both before and since that notice, similar ones have been published or sent to all Israeli men and to many, if not most, Israeli women, in accordance with the provisions of the most comprehensive and stringent draft and reserve duty law in the world.

This is the law which sends eighteen-year-old girls who have at least some high school education to the Army for twenty months, where they serve either in the Army itself, or as teachers in border villages, development towns, or city slums, or are seconded to the civilian police. It is the law that sometimes calls up even married women and mothers for reserve duty until they are about forty. It is the law that sends eighteen-year-old boys, regardless of educational background, to the Army for thirty-three months. It is the law that continues calling men up for as much as sixty days of reserve duty each and every year of their lives until they are about fifty. And when we speak of reserve duty, or what the Israelis call, *miluim,* we are speaking about assignments that can range from a soft job at General Staff Headquarters in Tel-Aviv—the Ministry of Defense and Zahal have not yet moved up to Jerusalem, as have other government departments—to placid patrols in the occupied West Bank of Jordan, or from shootouts with terrorists on the Syrian and Lebanese borders or in the Gaza Strip to open warfare and death on the Suez Canal.

In short, the Israeli military service law is one that can prompt one person writing in Zahal's magazine, *Bamachane (In the Camp),* a few days before the Six Day War, to call I s r a e l i s "soldiers-on-leave-eleven-months-of-the-year," and another person, a kibbutznik (or member of a collective settlement) talking to other kibbutzniks right after the War, to say: "This army is actually the nation, it belongs to the nation. And what the Army does, it doesn't do alone: the whole nation does it."

Without this kind of attitude, it would be impossible for a newly bereaved mother to say in 1967: "After all, what do I want? What am I complaining about? What am I crying about? That's how we brought my Nimrod up. It's we who brought our sons up to lay down their lives. What do I expect? It's we who prepared him for the moment of truth; this was the moment, and we knew that it would have to be paid for." Without this kind of attitude it would be impossible for most husbands and wives to accept *miluim* as ungrudgingly as they do.

After all, when a man goes on his annual reserve duty, it's not two weeks of the fun and games and extra income that characterize many National Guard and Reserve units in the United States. In Israel, *miluim* is a very serious business from which the part-time soldier may not return alive or well. Everyone goes—professors and students in the middle of the school year, the self-employed, those who work for others, newcomers, oldtimers. And when a man goes on *miluim,* despite the fact that in most cases his civilian salary is covered by National Insurance, it makes no difference that he is divorced or a widower caring for his children alone, or that he is leaving behind a sick child, an ailing parent, or a brand new bride. Judy Carr, writing in *The Israel Digest* of July 7, 1972, tells of a young bride who "saw herself as a romantic soldier's wife . . . but when her husband actually went on *miluim* leaving her sadly alone fearing for his life, she said: 'It was horrid. I don't want to be a heroine. Just give me my husband back again. If my husband were killed I would not feel heroic. I would curse Israel.' "

Despite the heavy personal burdens that regular and reserve service imposes on them, few Israelis want to change it in the absence of a real and permanent peace with their Arab neighbors, a peace which, for example, would allow Israelis to vacation freely in Beirut, Amman, or Cairo if they had the money and inclination to do so. The vast majority of them serve willingly—some of course do not—because *they* feel they must. It is this overwhelming feeling, not coercion, that makes the system work. That is the only way that any democratic system can work.

A few years ago the Israeli Army conducted a poll of seventeen-year-old high school boys. Among other things, it asked them if they would volunteer for military duty if there were no draft. Seventy percent said yes, twenty percent said they weren't sure, and only ten percent said no. At about the same time, when it seemed likely that the number of men eligible for the Army would exceed the Army's anticipated needs, there were proposals for changing from a universal to a more selective form of military service, but they were not accepted. Rather than eliminating compulsory conscription altogether, the country opted for shorter periods of universal service, if necessary, in order to preserve, in the words of Colonel Mordechai M. Bar-On, the then Chief Education Officer of Zahal, "the sacred principle of the universal draft."

Not only do young Israelis not shirk their military obligation, but they are perhaps the only young people in the world who beg, cajole, and even try to falsify facts in order not to be rejected from serving for, say, medical reasons. For in Israel, to be rejected for military service, especially if there is no good visible reason for it, is to be rejected from and by society itself, to be excommunicated, as it were, from your friends and peer-group. This is why one of the things that rankles the Israeli "Black Panthers," disadvantaged and discriminated against teenagers and young adults of North African and Middle Eastern Sephardic stock (who are not black and who have no connection with the American Black Panthers), is that they have a high military rejection rate. And they have such a high rate because they have very poor health profiles. They also have more juvenile delinquency, more serious police records, and worse mental health backgrounds than their fellow Israelis of Ashkenazic stock, who hail mostly from Europe, North and South America, the United Kingdom, and elsewhere.

The April 2, 1971 issue of the *Jerusalem Post* magazine section describes what happened to one of these young men, Reuven by name, when he reported for induction: "Then they asked me if I had a police record. I told them yes. They sent me to the psychiatrist. . . . Then they told me to go to room 8, where I was told that I wouldn't be accepted in the army. I was terribly hurt. I wanted to go to the army. Then I thought, well, I'll help my parents for the next two years instead." The article continues: "Reuven had made friends in his kibbutz days, whom he still saw. 'Some of them were girls and they were always asking me, "When are you going into the army?" I would always tell them that I'd got deferment because my father was ill, but how long can you keep on lying? In the end I grew ashamed and went back to my old friends in Musrara [a Jerusalem slum].' After that, Reuven's life is a sad and unedifying story of working at odd jobs, delinquency, smoking hashish, which he says has weakened him physically, and being outside of any society except that of the street gangs. . . . He would like to be a clerk . . . or a youth leader, but municipal or government offices [and many private enterprises as well] do not employ men rejected by the army."

On a more bizarre and, psychologically speaking, more tragic note, in that same year the same newspaper carried an item about an Isaac Rubinstein, apparently an Ashkenazic youth. He was so upset at his exclusion from the Army for health reasons that he wrote repeated letters of protest to General Haim Bar-Lev, the then Chief of Staff. When they brought no positive results, the poor lad managed to get himself arrested on the other side of the Lebanese frontier posing as an Israeli soldier.

2

The Sanctification
of the Army

MOST ISRAELIS ARE absolutely convinced that the only thing that stands between them and their destruction is their army. Having been traumatized by Adolf Hitler's extermination of one-third of the then total population of Jewry, having fought and won four wars for survival, and being determined that the sickening spectacle of unarmed Jews meekly going to their deaths will never happen again—certainly not in Israel—Israelis are very protective of their army and its image. They believe it to be a fair and humane army, even to its enemies, and do not take kindly to its being criticized.

Thus an organization called Daled Bet (the initial letters for the Hebrew words, Dikui Bogdim, which mean Suppression of Traitors) once circulated a flyer in Jerusalem. Directed against Israeli new leftists, it said in part: "You have been warned. . . . Stop your vile practice of dirtying the name of your country's security forces. . . . We will not stand by as you self-hating Jews use your freedom here to cast a bad name on Zahal. . . . " Nothing came of the episode. The organization, if it still exists, certainly does not represent the typical Israeli. But the warning did expose a raw nerve and it did find its way into the press as a news story and not as an advertisement.

Even as renowned an establishment figure as Foreign Minister Abba Eban has not been spared criticism from those who don't like to hear their sacred army scolded, no matter how gently. During a 1973 address at the University of Haifa on Mount Carmel, which dealt with some of the lesser qualities of his countrymen, Eban said: "In an essential air operation against murderous saboteurs, the inhabitants of a Druze village in Lebanon are inadvertently hit; and a great clamor of protest goes up precisely because the authorized representative of the government acknowledged the error and expressed regret." This immediately prompted Lea Ben-Dor, a well-known and respected journalist, who served as a Palestinian Jew in the British Army during World War II, to write an article in the *Jerusalem Post* called "Mr. Eban and the Ugly Israeli." Eban, she rejoined:

> . . . picked on some examples that are a little less than con-
> vincing. When civilians were accidentally hit in an attack
> on a terrorist camp in the Lebanon there was a clamor be-
> cause Mr. Allon, then Acting Premier (Mr. Eban did not
> mention him by name), ordered an apology for the mistake.
> Here Mr. Eban is being less than a seasoned politician, for
> the criticism was not directed at the regret for the loss of
> civilian lives, but at an obscure suggestion [by whom Miss
> Ben-Dor does not say] that Mr. Allon somehow regretted
> the incident more than the Army, and this at a time when
> Israel's forces were under sharp attack in the UN Security
> Council. Mr. Eban ascribes these and other acts of illiber-
> ality in part to the "imaginary assumption of weakness."

She then took off against Eban with the subtlety of a sledge-hammer:

Memories of 1948 [Israel's War of Independence], 1956 [the Sinai Campaign] and 1967 [the Six Day War] certainly lie at the back of the present Israeli aggressiveness. The army won these three wars and we could not have afforded to lose them. Can Mr. Eban guarantee there will not be another? And that we shall survive it, too, even if we forget our essential weakness, the smallness of Israel, and are no longer afraid to risk losing? Are we really already a strong nation that does not have to beat drums? We can afford a mistake in Africa, a wrong guess in France. Can we afford a reverse on a battlefield? Even if we can explain why it happened and was nobody's fault?

Despite their surprise and unhappiness at Intelligence and other Army shortcomings when the 1973 Yom Kippur War began, Israelis accord to Zahal a degree of devotion that is unique in the history of democratic societies. One could almost describe that devotion as sanctification. In fact, Rabbi Shlomo Goren, the present Ashkenazic Chief Rabbi of Israel, and for more than twenty years before that the Chief Chaplain of the Israeli Army, has used words and phrases closely akin to sanctification. After the Six Day War he called Zahal's members "soldiers of Israel, beloved of your people," and "beloved soldiers, dear sons of your people." Some time later he said: "Our goal . . . is to link our defense forces with the Maccabees and Bar Kochba, with Joshua and David. The Torah says," Rabbi Goren continued, " 'Let your camp be holy.' " And Ruth Bondy, the senior editor of the book about Israel called *Mission Survival,* has this poignant passage in it. "An old man is pushing a baby carriage. His wife struggles along after him, pausing to embrace a soldier. 'You are our Messiahs,' " she suddenly says to him.

In that same book there is also this passage: "They all have a great name now—*Giborei Israel*—the heroes of Israel. Zahal is the modern name. *Giborei Israel*—those were the warriors under King David, those were the Maccabees, those were the people of Massada and the rebels of the Warsaw Ghetto.

That is what we call them today. There is a greatness in the name. . . ."

Messiahs or not, Maccabees or not, the practical result of this feeling toward Zahal is that no group of Israelis, including the politicians who wield great power and the professors who enjoy great prestige, possess the esteem, the love, and the post-retirement career opportunities that accrue almost automatically to the Army's senior officer corps from the rank of lieutenant-colonel upward.

Not even the venerated kibbutz, the ideological fixative of the Zionist movement, can compete with the Army in this regard. The kudos which older Israelis give to the pioneering kibbutz for *building* the state, younger Israelis give to the pragmatic Army for *preserving* the state. There is, however, a tie between these two institutions. For the number of kib-butzniks in the officer corps and in such elite units as the Air Force and the paratroops is much higher than their three to four percent of Israel's present population, a point painfully illustrated by the fact that a quarter of the officers killed and wounded in the 1967 war were kibbutzniks. Additionally, most of the members of Nahal, the Army's unique corps of Fighting Pioneer Youth, who mix military with agricultural duties, are kibbutzniks or would-be kibbutzniks.

There are, in Israel, daily reminders of the great popular respect—perhaps there is too much of it—for the Army and its soldiers. It is a respect which some people and parties use for grinding their own personal and political axes. What are some examples, beyond those already given, of this great out-pouring of feeling for Zahal?

There is, for instance, this episode which I personally witnessed when I was living in Jerusalem. One of my neighbors, and not my friendliest one at that, suddenly stopped me in the street in front of my apartment one day. With great joy and emotion she told me that her son had just been accepted into the Israeli Air Force as a flight cadet. She is the wife of an Israeli academic, a most prestigious profession in Israel. Yet she stopped me and anyone else who cared to listen to tell them about "my son the Air Force pilot," which in Israel is a much greater source of Jewish parental pride than "my son the doctor" or "my son the professor."

Then there is the 1971 petition presented to Avraham Harman, President of The Hebrew University of Jerusalem, the nation's leading institution of higher learning. It called for admission preference for soldiers finished with their compulsory service. Composed and distributed on the campus by the Jerusalem student branch of Gahal, the principal right-wing opposition party in Israel, the petition said:

> We, the undersigned, students of The Hebrew University of Jerusalem, are distressed over the fact that discharged soldiers seeking admission to the University are rejected, in place of applicants who through various excuses, purposely evaded service in Zahal.

> We demand that discharged soldiers be placed at the top of the priority list of those admitted to the University—without of course ignoring the minimal standard required of every person applying for admission to an academic institution.

A similar use of Zahal's name and popularity for partisan political purposes occurred at about the same time when a group opposed to the methods and style of the American-imported J.D.L.—the Jewish Defense League—circulated a flyer in Jerusalem. Its principal argument was that Israelis don't need the J.D.L. since Zahal "fulfills the task of defending us with efficiency."

Or from another vantage point, there is the following 1963 reaction by General Ezer Weizman, then head of the Air Force, to a newsman's question as to whether Air Force men were being attracted to civil aviation careers:

> That sort we regard as having been spun out by centrifugal force. We've got nothing against them—but we don't want any of their favors. Anybody who wants to leave—let him

go to El Al, let him carry 100 passengers on the Lydda-U.S. route, let him collect his 2,000 pounds a month, and may he have a long and happy life. But whoever wants excitement, new challenges, class Double-A-De-Luxe satisfaction, and—I'm not ashamed to say it—on top of it all wants to be a pioneer, then he's welcome to the Air Force. Training one pilot costs us—costs you . . . half a million. And if the fellow picks himself up and goes to the civilian market—well, if you call that logic, then it beats me what logic is!

In sum, it is the young people, the very ones who have to do most of the fighting and dying, who are especially impressed with Zahal. They are impressed with how it relates to them, with how it reflects them, and with how it separates them from some of the mores of their elders. As Amnon Rubinstein, writing in *Ha'aretz,* the *New York Times* of Israel, put it in 1967:

As against the petrified doctrines of these men of yesterday, the contemporary Israeli is marked by a pragmatic approach. The Israeli Army is led by young men of this type. These are men who set themselves an objective, attacked it effectively, rapidly, skillfully, and reached their objective by the best possible means. All the deficiencies to be found in the veteran political leadership—historic rights, petrified dogmatism, lack of contact with the people, language and style dating from the past—do not exist in Israel Army leadership. Only in the army is the new Israeli generation permitted to talk its own language, to do its job in the way it understands. And we may say that the results of this attempt are not so very bad.

3

The Detractors

ZAHAL DOES HAVE its Israeli detractors and draft evaders, however. They are found chiefly among young men and women who take advantage of liberally interpreted exemptions on religious grounds, even though pacifism has never been a tenet of Judaism and warfare under a variety of circumstances is both permitted and required under *halacha* (Jewish religious law). This will be discussed in the chapter on religion and the Army.

As for draft refusals on non-religious grounds, there have been a few young men who have claimed that right without success. In the summer of 1971, for instance, for the first time in the country's history, four young men returned their induction notices. In a letter to Defense Minister Moshe Dayan, they wrote: "We were not born free in order to be oppressors and oppression's not a reason to die." They wrote further: "We are not prepared to do to another nation [presumably the Arabs in the occupied areas] what was done to our parents and ancestors."

Of these four, as of the end of that year, one changed his mind and joined Zahal, one was jailed for three weeks and then was drafted, one had as yet no action taken against him, and the fourth was Giora Neumann of Ramat-Aviv, a suburb of Tel-Aviv. His case became a bit of a cause célèbre in Israel.

Rather than refuse to enter the Army and fight his case as a civilian in a civil court, Neumann accepted induction but then refused to complete the induction procedures. Specifically, he would not take the oath of allegiance to Zahal. The Army had agreed to his offer to do non-military alternative service in a hospital or settlement within the so-called Green Line, the pre-1967 borders of Israel, but only if only he would take the oath and thus acknowledge the Army's jurisdiction over him. This he steadfastly would not do, not on the grounds of conscientious objection, but rather on the grounds that Zahal was an "army of occupation" engaged in measures of repression against inhabitants of the West Bank and the Golan Heights in general and of the Gaza Strip in particular. After serving five, thirty-five-day terms in the stockade for refusing five times to obey the order of an officer to complete the induction procedure, he was finally brought to military trial in May 1972.

In the end, in July 1972, he was sentenced to prison for eight months. Some of the points made in the verdict are interesting and illustrative of Zahal's perception in Israel. First, the military court said that no attempt was made by Neumann or his attorney to substantiate, as opposed to merely stating, their charges against Zahal. Second, the court said that Neumann "had exploited the courtroom to voice shameful and baseless attacks on the State and its army. Third, it held that the freedom of conscience claimed by Neumann and guaranteed to all Israelis "does not grant him immunity from the obligation of obeying the laws of the Knesset [Israel's Parliament], which are the expression of the will of the people." Fourth, the court refused to concede that the oath of allegiance was "unessential." In the words of the *Jerusalem Post's* account of the sentencing in its issue of July 18, 1972, the court held that "taking the oath was not only the soldier's first duty upon being inducted, but he is bound to observe it, 'whether he believes in it or not.'"

Each of us can decide for himself whether eight months is a long sentence. (Neumann's lawyer asked for a fine or a token penalty of a day in jail; the law allowed the court to send him to jail for as much as three years.) But the military prosecutor's reasoning was instructive especially in view of the debate in the United States over what to do about American deserters and draft dodgers during the Vietnam War. "A light penalty," he argued, "would be an affront to the thousands who not only fulfill their military obligations without demur but also through conviction that Israel cannot exist without Zahal."

Another draft refusal case that occurred at the same time involved Roger Deerhy, a thirty-one-year-old Moroccan Jew, who, after living in Paris for a while, came to Israel after the 1967 war. A permanent member of a kibbutz in the western Negev—the Negev refers to the whole of southern Israel from about Beersheba downward—he failed to report for his pre-induction examination because he was "against war and against serving in an army of occupation." When someone asked him what he would do if Israel were militarily attacked again, he replied: "I don't know. If I were personally in danger, I would probably defend myself." Before his six-months' jail sentence was announced, he told the court that he felt his case should be dismissed so that "I may live and work according to my conscience." Yuval Ronen's is the most recent instance of conscientious objection by an Israeli. In August 1973 he turned up in Oslo and asked Norwegian authorities for asylum because Israel was "waging an imperialist war" and, he told reporters, "I refuse to persecute people or chase them from their homes."

While the Neumann, Deerhy, and Ronen cases are interesting and newsworthy, they are hardly typical. Available figures since July 1970 show that only nine Israelis claimed conscientious objection—and four of them later changed their minds. It is thus difficult to gainsay former Chief of Staff General Haim Bar-Lev who has remarked that "if we compare this number with the hundreds of handicapped men who come to us and demand to be called up, I think we shall see the matter in a much more correct proportion."

This is not to say that there aren't young Israelis, some of them prominent in their own right or the sons of prominent parents, who voice serious criticisms of the Army, even though they serve in it. Amos Kollek, author of the novel *Don't Ask Me If I Love* and the son of Teddy Kollek, the Mayor of Jerusalem, has said: "I think three years of compulsory service is excessive. One year would be sufficient to teach the skills and exercise discipline." (The Army General Staff's rejoinder is that with the very sophisticated equipment now in its arsenal, training takes about a year and a half and that a shorter service period would mean that soldiers would leave when they are efficient, with a resultant drop in the country's overall military effectiveness.) Amos Kollek has also said that he hates "the strict regimentation and the absolute impersonality. My service has kept me from things I enjoy, but . . . I do recognize my obligation to my country and do not shirk it."

An even more outspoken critic is the Israeli playwright Amos Kenan. His 1970 satire *Queen of the Bathtub*, which Moshe Dayan called "toilet humor," closed under pressure after only twenty performances. Supposedly, according to the January 8, 1973 European edition of *Time*, this was "because it dealt brutally with Israeli losses during the 'war of attrition'" with Egypt. In 1973 his satire called *Jesus, As Seen By His Friends* played only seven times before Levi Guery, Israel's official government censor, closed it down. Despite the fact that Jesus is mentioned only once—in the title—Guery's explanation was that he found it "offensive to another religion."

But there are those, including Kenan, who believe that the real reason was his attacks on Israeli society, particularly the Army. He feels that "no longer do Jews swear by their intellectuals, by their rebels or their revolutionaries, but by their army and their soldiers. They do not want to be martyrs. They want to be an efficient people." So in one scene of *Jesus, As*

Seen By His Friends he has an Israeli housewife say: "Yester-day I noticed that my maid doesn't dust the table properly. So I called in the army. Now the army keeps things in order at home. It's a real delight to see how they rub, like well-oiled machines. My husband turned out to be inefficient too, so I called in the army. . . . The synagogues are more efficient now. The Dead Sea is more efficient. The Wailing Wall is more efficient. Even happiness is more efficient. But what pleases me most is that the army has become God. Now God is more efficient too." Perhaps the problem is not that the Army is so efficient, but that the rest of Israel is, relatively speaking, so inefficient.

In any case, the 1970 and 1973 episodes are not the only publicly expressed examples of Kenan's views. In a January 1972 interview in *Hayom* (Hebrew for *Today*), the English-language journal of the Philadelphia Union of Jewish Students, Kenan said that "there is social repression in Israel." Then, in an exchange of questions and answers with his interviewer, he linked some of this repression to Zahal:

Q: Could you be explicit? Could you give some examples?

A: It's very simple. From the age of eighteen until the age of fifty-five the Israeli is a soldier. So suppose you are forty-five. Suppose you are fifty. You are somebody. You are a professor or a bank manager, or whatever you like to be. From time to time they call you to a military office, just to check. Just to sign your name. But that's enough. The moment you enter the military office you are no longer a professor or a bank manager. You are nothing. You are a soldier, and that's all. You are under military jurisdiction. Even if it's only for fifteen minutes. For fifteen minutes you are again a soldier as you were when you were eighteen. And that's enough to put you in your proper place. That's enough. You don't need more than that. You don't need more apparant [*sic*] means of repression. That alone puts you in line.

Q: Would you say the Israeli army is more similar to a professional army, as in Canada or Great Britain, or closer to the Chinese model of a "peoples army?"

A: It's neither one nor the other. It could be adequately described as a popular army. Only the picture is not so nice because there are classes in Israel; there is an upper class and there is a lower class. The professional or standing army is the upper class; the reserve army is the lower class.

Q: What about dissent within the army, such as when there was a big outcry from within the army itself about the brutality in Gaza? Was that typical or was that an exception?

A: It's typical. It's not an exception. They try hard to maintain certain values, certain humanism. It becomes harder and harder to maintain it, but a decent effort is made.

What is interesting, indeed exciting, about this Kenan interview is not the obvious contradiction between his opinions of the army in his first and last answers. It is not his "discovery" that Israel has distinct social and economic classes. It is not even his error in both believing and stating that the reserves are for the lower classes. (Perhaps he meant to say that many of the non-commissioned and junior officers who make the Army their career are from the lower socio-economic, that is, Sephardic, elements.) What is interesting is that his views, more extreme than most other Israelis', do point up the new materialism and restlessness that come from a long military occupation that most young people did not expect. After their smashing 1967 victory, what they expected was a quick and final once-and-for-all peace. As one *sabra* (literally a cactus plant but figuratively the Hebrew word for a native-born Israeli) put it: "The younger generation in this country does not believe in the eternal Jewish fate of suffering. They don't want to fight all the time; they want to live, too."

33

One result of the unexpectedly long occupation of Arab territory has been some criticism and censure of Zahal's behavior, especially in the Gaza Strip in 1970 and 1971, when the Arabs living in the Strip were killing each other off at an alarming rate. Army personnel there were caught between the rocks and the hard place as Arab terrorists vented their anger and frustration at other Arabs who tried to live peacefully and even to work within Israel. Never having been trained for police duty, riot control, and a long military occupation of heavily populated and angered Arabs, Zahal was, on the one hand, blamed for not doing enough about the intra-Arab carnage. On the other hand, when it took steps that led to a lower rate of terror in the Strip, certain elements in Israel and abroad quickly accused it of "inhumane activities." (The famous French writer Jean-Paul Sartre, for example, called Zahal "an army of aggression.")

Adding to the confusion and the complaints was the role of the Israeli Border Police. The Border Police are not part of the Army. Instead they function under the Police Ministry. Many of their members are not Jews but Druzes whose religion is different from that of Orthodox Arabs. Since the creation of Israel, they cast their lot with the Jews. In any case, it is the Border Police that is mainly responsible for internal security in the occupied areas, or, in the Israeli phrase, the Administered Territories. It is the Border Police that patrols the borders and border villages of "Old Israel." When one reads about running fights and shootouts between the Israeli security forces and Arab terrorists and saboteurs, the Israelis involved are more often than not members of the Border Police and not the Army. Yet Army units are sometimes involved too. And when one realizes that in the Gaza Strip the uniforms and helmets of the two groups are hardly distinguishable, that in order to be sure who is riding in whose jeep, one must take the trouble to notice whether the vehicle is carrying Police or Army license tags, one sees how tangled the situation can become.

Nevertheless, be it Border Police or Army, it is true that there have been excesses in the Strip and that some of them have involved Zahal. In February 1971 charges were brought against one officer and ten men for the unprovoked roughing up of residents there, including women. Other officers, of higher rank, were reprimanded for failing to issue clear orders that would have prevented such behavior in the first place. There were at least three cases of looting by Israeli soldiers, who were punished. So great was the uproar within Israel herself that the Army spokesman made the above facts known in an official press conference attended by the Army Chief of Staff. And Defense Minister Moshe Dayan made an unusually detailed statement about them in the Israeli Parliament. Dayan noted that soldiers on curfew duty needed and would get better training and supervision. He deplored that in a number of cases, houses which were not under any special suspicion were damaged unnecessarily. And he announced that the Chief of Staff, Lieutenant General Haim Bar-Lev, had ordered that physical violence against civilians was to be used carefully, and, then, only to maintain curfews and not to punish for punishment's sake. General Bar-Lev also ordered a more clear rewriting of standing orders on curfew enforcement so as to eliminate misinterpretation as much as possible.

The *Jerusalem Post* is a newspaper often reflecting the views of the Israeli government. Because it is published in English, an important access language to the outside world, its somewhat defensive and deferential reaction to the above events has significance for what it tells us about how Israel perceives—and would like the outside world to perceive—negative episodes involving her Army. On February 11, 1971 the *Post* wrote:

> The Army's quick and resolute action in investigating complaints about the behavior of troops during a search in one of the Gaza Strip refugee camps is to be highly commended.

> There was no attempt to conceal the facts even though it was to be expected that incidents of this nature could only serve Egyptian propaganda—and, indeed, Cairo was

quick to seize the opportunity and addressed a note to the Security Council. The Army has wisely decided to view such improper conduct with the utmost seriousness, as undermining discipline, morale and the good name of the Israeli soldier. It stressed that acts that might be routine in other parts of the world during search operations are not acceptable to the Israeli Army. As a result of the incident the Army will shortly lay down new guidelines for soldiers entrusted with the task of maintaining order in Gaza. There will even be special sessions with sociologists and psychologists.

Damage has been repaired and compensation paid, but this does not, of course, solve the problems of the Gaza Strip. Unlike the situation in the West Bank, almost two-thirds of the Gaza population are refugees living in camps with very limited sources of income. In addition to this basic socio-economic problem, there remained in Gaza after the Six Day War hundreds of soldiers who had been attached to Palestinian units operating under Egyptian command.

There are considerable quantities of weapons in the area, while the population density and refugee camp environment make terrorist activity easier and the task of the local police and the Israeli Army infinitely more difficult. In recent months scores of Arab residents were killed or injured, including women and children. The local authorities under the Egyptian-appointed Mayor failed to stem the terror.

Another example of the Israeli habit of first admitting that Zahal has the right to do something, and then half-heartedly deploring the way in which that right was exercised is the Akraba case, which occurred in the summer of 1971. Akraba is a small West Bank hamlet near Nablus and the Jordan River. One day the Army sprayed and destroyed about 125 acres of the villagers' crops. When querried about this in the Cabinet, Defense Minister Dayan said that Zahal's action was approved by the appropriate Army commanders, but that he himself thought the decision to destroy the crops chemically was a "wrong one." Dayan also said that the land in question was a training site which the Army had expropriated "many years ago" and that it had repeatedly warned the Arab farmers not to cultivate the land there. Yet they did so anyway.

Then there is the 1972 Rafiah affair. Intertwined in that episode was a combination of factors including the Jews, the Arabs, military censorship in democratic Israel, the government's ambivalent attitude toward the future of the Administered Territories, and the Army's operational freedom within these territories.

Basically, the affair involved the Army's forced evacuation of Bedouins living near the southern end of the Gaza Strip. It also involved the fencing off of the evacuated land and the Army's refusal to allow the affected Bedouins—some six thousand of them—to return. The military reason given for these actions was that the land was being used as a terrorist infiltration route. But there may well have been another motive, of higher political significance, concerning the ultimate demarcation, disposition, and demography of the conquered lands. There are those in Israel who believe that the Rafiah area must eventually be settled permanently with many, many Jews who would serve as a human buffer between the heavily Arab-populated Gaza Strip and the lightly Bedouin-populated Northern Sinai. It is therefore possible, if not probable, that the government "used" the Army to get out of a public relations and public opinion predicament.

Specifically, the government reprimanded the senior officer connected with the Rafiah evacuation, saying that he acted without prior authorization. But what really rankled the government was not the "unauthorized" action. Rather it was the fact that it was done so quickly and effectively that it alarmed local Arabs and certain segments of public opinion at home and abroad. Perhaps this is why the government refused to name the senior officer who was reprimanded or to disclose the exact nature of his reprimand.

When Moshe Dayan was asked about the Rafiah affair in

an interview over the Army radio, he gave this rather interesting reply:

> Q. What lessons have been learned from the affair of the Rafiah salient, and why were reports withheld from the public?

> Dayan: A person has to act according to orders. There were actions not according to orders, even if those who decided on these actions had the best of intentions. But approval had not been obtained.

> I do not think that, in principle, it is absolutely forbidden to move inhabitants. It is sometimes necessary and permissable to move Jewish and Arab residents in the territories and outside them. But if the action is justified it can be taken only on the basis of a decision by the competent authorities; if it is for security needs, then on the basis of a decision of the General Staff, and if it is for other needs—on the basis of a government decision.

Dayan did not say whether the decision in this case was a security one, a political one, or a combined one. But on the question of withholding the information from the public, he displayed that overly broad approach that characterizes Israel's definition of military security, an approach which most of his countrymen agree with. For he said:

> The entire question of withholding publicity belongs to a different category of question and that is—when should the army publish certain files or certain information and when should it not do so? On Rafiah, discussions and publicity were not prevented. The evidence is clear enough. The press deals with it whenever it wants, journalists write what they like. But the demand that everything written in that file be released for publication, including the names of those concerned, was rejected. On security issues the decision whether to publish or not should be based on security considerations and should be subject to the laws of the state.

When PORI, Public Opinion Research of Israel, Ltd., asked a sample of the Israeli public in May 1972, "Do you justify or not the evacuation of the Bedouins from the Rafiah area?," approximately sixty-two percent said yes, thirty percent said no, seven percent said they had never heard of the matter, and one percent said they didn't know. (For exact breakdowns of this and other poll results in this book, see Appendix 3.) When, during the same week, PORI asked, "Should or shouldn't the name of the high-ranking officer who was censured by the General Army Staff on the Rafiah Bedouins evacuation be disclosed?," sixty-five percent said no, almost sixteen percent said yes, eighteen percent didn't know anything about the matter, and one percent didn't answer.

Israel has a State Comptroller's Office, headed for years by the highly respected Dr. Yitzchak E. Nebenzahal. Similar to the General Accounting Office in the United States, it is, in the language of the official *Israel Government Year Book*, "responsible for the supreme audit of the Ministries, the Defense establishment, State enterprises and institutions, corporations and companies in whose management the Government shares, bodies placed under inspection by a Law, a Knesset [Parliament] decision or agreement with the Government, and all local authorities. The State Comptroller's status, operations and powers are governed by the State Comptroller's Law . . . and his inspections are designed to ascertain whether that Law, and the principles of economy, efficiency and moral integrity which it enjoins, have been observed." Our interest in the State Comptroller, who is also Israel's ombudsman, or Complaints Commissioner, is confined to what he has said and done about the defense establishment.

In March 1971, when newsmen asked him whether he was more strict or less strict in checking defense matters than those connected with other ministries and agencies, he replied that he was more strict because he and his employees were the *only* ones in the country who could look into Defense Ministry operations that were not known or announced to the general public. A month later, when his Twenty-first Annual Report was published, there was what the *Jerusalem Post* called "relatively mild criticism of the defense establishment." For example, he found fault with the fact that for the second year in a row the defense authorities had exceeded their budget by almost $65 million. He objected to the fact that one batch of military items ordered from local sources (to avoid paying precious foreign currency to foreign suppliers) had been "linked" to the foreign manufacturers' prices. He urged greater caution in fixing the terms between the Defense Ministry and its local suppliers. In particular did he object to the practice of putting thirty percent down when the order was placed and paying the rest within sixty days of delivery.

Zahal itself, as differentiated from the Ministry of Defense, was criticized for inefficiency in maintaining "fighting equipment." The Military Government was criticized for paying architectural and engineering fees for a wider road than was actually built between the Israeli port of Eilat and occupied Sharm el-Sheikh, at the tip of the Sinai Penninsula. Dr. Nebenzahl also criticized the way some loans to inhabitants of the Gaza Strip were handled by the military, although the man involved was later charged with taking bribes. The Comptroller also found sloppy checking of what the Israeli military calls health profiles. As a result, older reservists were not reposted to other units and jobs better suited to their lower states of health. He also criticized Army Welfare units for sometimes failing to inform soldiers of their privileges and rights concerning extra pay and other benefits available to them under certain conditions.

The Comptroller's report mentioned no names and referred to things in a general way. But it created a great stir anyway. In an editorial headed "Comptroller's Shocking Document," the *Post* wrote on April 22, 1971: "Three years ago, the State Comptroller complained that vestiges of Ottoman administrative practices still prevail in Israel and called attention to the fact that a modern country cannot be run along such lines. Dr. Nebenzahl has now tabled even more serious accusations, some close to corruption." Specifically, the editorial deplored that at a time when Israel was having problems with slums, poverty, juvenile delinquency, crime, drugs, and insufficient schools, hospitals, and housing, "we discover how the government, and particularly the Treasury and the Ministry of Defense seem to be wasting large sums through ill management." The State Comptroller, the editorial continued, "has done a valuable public service by not mincing words when it came to describing the new attitude of officials to the public funds. They no longer see themselves as trustees for the taxes we pay and the funds Jews contribute to this country." Pressing its point, the *Post* went on: "It is the general approach of spend and spend and spend that prevails, and if we do not combat this attitude among our officials, this country will be heading into more social unrest than it is witnessing at present. Israel . . . cannot afford the luxury of waste and financial reglect. This breeds lawlessness and apathy which a society under siege cannot permit." Finally, pointing its heaviest guns directly at the biggest users of Israeli taxes, the newspaper said: "The government cannot plead defense costs when it comes to argue its case. Neither can it blame untrained officials. The Ministry of Finance employs some of the best economists in the country and the Ministry of Defense some of the best engineers and cost analysts available."

In his 1972 report the State Comptroller took a different tack. Acknowledging that it was the Knesset's Finance Committee and not the military authorities that decides what information should be deleted for security reasons from any of his published documents, Dr. Nebenzahl wrote: "I am glad to say that secrecy is not used as an excuse for concealing mistakes." But, he went on, "The trouble is that we are the only civilian agency which has admission to defense affairs at the workaday level. Is it fair to the military authorities themselves to leave them so much autonomy and self-sufficiency in an area that comprises over one-fifth of the national income?" While the Comptroller had no objections at all that soldiers should be making the operational decisions and choices regarding weapons and related matters, he could not see why on matters of administration and costs, the defense establishment, including Zahal itself, should be exempted from the same scrutiny that he gives to civilian public bodies in Israel.

As for the year 1973, the Army portion of the State Comptroller's report was far from complimentary. Dr. Nebenzahl was critical of inefficiencies in the Quartermaster Branch. He was critical of the Army's failure to live up to the requirements of a 1966 decision to modernize its methods of inventory control. He found that maintenance standards in the Armored Corps had fallen below the necessary minimums, that vehicles were not always serviced and overhauled when they were supposed to be, and when they were, it took too long. Recruitment offices were chastised for their red tape, military courts for "administrative deficiencies," and the Army as a whole for its losing, misplacing, or damaging "huge amounts" of supplies and equipment. Clearly, Dr. Nebenzahl was becoming bolder and bolder in his criticism of the military with each passing year.

But what caused the most fury, and even mystery, about the 1973 Comptroller's report, as compared with the ones in previous years, were revelations, and reactions to the revelations, of large-scale looting immediately after the Six Day War. For this was the report which disclosed for the first time that millions of dollars worth of Sinai-based *civilian* equipment and property had been systematically taken away perhaps before the military was able to establish effective control of the huge Sinai Peninsula. (The government's policy of reclaiming, removing, refurbishing, and incorporating into Zahal's arsenal usable Soviet and Egyptian military equipment has never been an issue.)

This was also the report to whose full publication the Defense Ministry had no objection, but not so the Israel Attorney-General. He insisted on the deletion of two pages. According to the *Jerusalem Post* of March 27, 1973, he did not want the pages withheld on security grounds but rather on the grounds that "they might impair Israel's relations with foreign countries whose property was involved." "It would seem," said the *Post*, "that the two offending pages describe how the government authorities responsible for Sinai allowed the removal of equipment worth millions of dollars by State corporations, and point out the failure of the authorities to take care of the equipment or probe later where it was hauled off to, and why. It was this conduct on the part of the authorities which the Attorney-General apparently regarded as potentially harmful to foreign relations—rather than the fact of the stealing itself." Curiously, there is nothing in the public record that shows any concern by Foreign Minister Abba Eban or any of his subordinates about the foreign repercussions of the Sinai looting. Also, it may or may not be significant that the Attorney-General in question, retired Colonel Meir Shamgar, was for some seven years the Judge-Advocate-General of Zahal, and that his last post before becoming the Attorney-General of the Ministry of Justice was that of Legal Advisor to the Ministry of Defense.

In any event, one of the few prominent Israelis to mention Zahal *by name* in the looting debate that swept the nation was Dr. Yochanan Bader, a member of the Knesset's Finance Committee representing Gahal, the principal right-wing opposition party to Israel's ruling Labor Alignment. Referring to the missing mining equipment, drilling equipment, heavy electrical equipment, etc., he asked: "What happened to the property?" There is no doubt, he said, "that almost all of it disappeared and that there were errors by the army, government institutions and companies, and private thefts as well." And so there were. For how so much heavy equipment could be moved so far from the depths of the Sinai Peninsula to the interior of Israel and concealed for so long a time is indeed a mystery.

There was also shock and surprise in the country when Israelis learned that some few members of their beloved Zahal looted the wreckage of the Libyan passenger jet that was mistakenly shot down by the Israeli Air Force in 1973. But as soon as the General Staff learned about it, which was almost immediately, it court-martialed and punished the four soldiers found guilty.

Israel has even had her own "My-Lai," with the terribly important difference, when one compares it to the American My-Lai massacre in Vietnam in 1969, that it was never covered up. Punishment was meted out to the guilty regardless of rank, without any hemming and hawing. It happened back in 1956 on the very first day of the Sinai Campaign. When that war broke out, the Army ordered a 5 P.M. to 6 A.M. curfew in Arab border villages. The Border Police was ordered by Zahal to enforce it strictly, with gunfire if necessary. A group of unfortunate Israeli-Arab inhabitants of Kfar Kasim—men, women, and children—left their village before the announcement of the curfew. They thus knew nothing of its existence or its penalties. When the Border Police spotted them returning to the village later in the day, the commander in charge, a Major Shmuel Malinki asked for instructions from the Army's regional commander, a Colonel Issachar Shadmi. The latter replied enigmatically: "May Allah have mercy on their souls." The former took this to mean "Fire upon them" and he did so, killing forty-three and wounding fourteen totally innocent people.

In contrast to our own My Lai, which took about two years to come to light, the Israeli government ordered an investigation two days later. Six weeks after that, the then Prime Minister David Ben-Gurion told the Parliament about it. As he put it, they were "coming home in all innocence." He announced the payment of compensation and the forthcoming courts-martial of all those responsible. And indeed all those responsible were punished. Roughly, the higher the rank the harsher the punishment. While the court found that none of the guilty had actually initiated an illegal order, it held them all culpable for obeying one.

Not only did this episode mark, in the words of Robert C. Toth, writing in the April 26, 1971 Paris edition of the *Herald Tribune*, "the first time an unvanquished democracy prosecuted and convicted its own military for mass murder of unarmed civilians." It also marks "the first time," in the words of an Israeli government statement, that "the tradition of complete, unquestioned obedience in the [Israeli] armed forces was discussed, defined and limited. . . . The judgment restricted the rights of officers and soldiers and limited the application of force against civilians. . . . The soldier . . . is not above the law. It is his duty to refuse to obey, and to resist carrying out, a manifestly illegal order or action."

What all of this adds up to is this. While Zahal is a humane army, as armies go, and its moral standards may well be, as most Israelis believe, the highest in the world, they are not as high as those of the angels. Even the bravest knights have their blemishes; the shiniest and strongest suits of armor, their chinks.

This is why there is now an Army ombudsman, retired Chief of Staff Haim Laskov, for Dr. Nebenzahl, in his capacity as Israel's civilian ombudsman, is prohibited by law from handling complaints against the military. This is why Premier Golda Meir has spoken of "regrettable deviations" and "painful irregularities" by Zahal in the occupied territories. This is why Defense Minister Moshe Dayan has promised to take steps to avoid the exercise of "bad judgment" by Army officers in the territories. And this is also why, in an article headed "Israel to Tighten Reign on the Military," the New York Times' Peter Grose wrote from Jerusalem in July 1972: "Behind the cautious official statements was the long-standing fear of many Israelis, as well as foreign observers, that a successful army would begin to forget the official policy of tact and sensitivity in day-to-day dealings with the Arab populations that came under Israeli control in the 1967 war."

On balance, Zahal has not forgotten. But the longer the occupation lasts, the greater will be the temptation to forget. It is the government's duty to see to it that Zahal never forgets.

4

The "Administered" Territories

THE ISRAELIS SINCERELY believe that theirs is the most benign occupation in all of history. It probably is. And the vast majority of conquered Arabs in the Golan Heights, the Gaza Strip, the Jordanian West Bank, the Sinai Desert, and East Jerusalem (the only piece of captured land that the Israelis have actually annexed and incorporated into their capital city) would privately agree with them.

But make no mistake about it. The Arabs detest the occupation and the occupiers. When a Christian tourist spending his first night in an East Jerusalem hotel asked the bellhop "In which direction is Jordan?," the latter replied indignantly: "Sir, this is Jordan!" By its very definition, a military occupation, no matter how "gentle," is a symbol and reminder of defeat, in this case by a numerically inferior but technologically superior enemy. For a proud people like the Arabs, who dream of past glories in prior centuries, the occupation reinforces their frustrating and humiliating inability to meet the twentieth century on its own modern terms. Thus, psychologically speaking, it matters little to them whether the occupation is harsh or humane, although on a practical day-to-day basis they are quite capable of appreciating the difference.

From the Israeli viewpoint, there is more than semantics involved in the words they use to label the captured lands over which they now rule, lands that are more than three times larger than the area of pre-1967 Israel. Among themselves they use the Hebrew words *hashstachim hamuchzakim,* which mean "the occupied territories" or "the held territories." But they always translate those words for foreigners as "the administered territories." There are reasons for this. The latter term presumably lessens the negative connotations associated with the word "occupied." Also, the Israelis believe (or hope) that the use of the former term keeps their options open at the negotiating table. (Incidentally, in this matter of word usage, the Israelis never refer to armed Arab resisters as "guerrillas" or "commandos." They believe that such words are much too flattering and noble to be applied to men unwilling or unable to face Zahal and the Border Police on the formal field of battle. Instead they refer to them as "terrorists" or "saboteurs.")

The fact that Zahal had no operational doctrine or organized units to deal with the governance of enemy civilians is proof that the length of the present occupation was almost totally unexpected. There are two reasons for this. First, the Israelis did not expect King Hussein of Jordan to intervene, just as he did not in the Sinai Campaign with Egypt in 1956. Second, after three stunning victories—in 1948, 1956, and 1967—they actually believed that the Arabs would quickly make peace this time, obviating the need for a long occupation and its accompanying administrative machinery. But of course they were wrong. They underestimated Arab intransigence. Suddenly they found themselves ruling a million Arabs from three countries: Syria, Jordan, and Egypt.

The chain of command is from the Cabinet to the Defense Minister to Major General Shlomo Gazit, who carries the title Coordinator of Government Operations in the Administered

Areas, Ministry of Defense, and Head of the Military Government Department of the G Branch of the General Staff. In
the words of the official *Israel Government Year Book*, he pos-
sesses "the authority for all aspects of coordination and integration with the [other] Ministries concerned." Again in the
words of the *Year Book*, "the overriding policy is minimum
interference with the internal conduct . . . of the lives of the
inhabitants." Or as Brigadier General Rafael Vardi, the Military Governor of Judea and Samaria (the Israeli designation
for Jordan's West Bank), told me on Christmas Eve of 1972,
"we let the orchestra conduct itself."

The steps in the implementation of this policy are the
following. First, get the essential services working. Second,
use as many of the former Arab personnel and as much of the
former legal and administrative apparatus as possible. Third,
keep a low Israeli profile, especially militarily. Fourth, intervene with force only when absolutely necessary, and then only
as quickly as possible, for the shortest period possible, and
with the smallest number of men possible. In effect, the Army
rules through the Arab mayors and municipal councillors, or
the "Notables" as they are often called in the Middle East. And
the low Israeli profile really exists and really works.

In the many times I visited the occupied areas, I saw very
few Israeli soldiers and policemen. They were there and they
would make their presence visible whenever they had to, but I
just never saw many of them moving about. Take the huge
Sinai Peninsula, for example. Its 23,622 square miles makes it
about equal in size to the state of West Virginia or to the
combined areas of Massachusetts, Rhode Island, New Jersey,
and Delaware. On one of the days that President Anwar Sadat
of Egypt had set for renewed hostilities, my wife, my daughter,
and I joined a group of Israelis for a week of traveling and
camping in the vast occupied region. Yet despite Sadat's
threat and except only for the troops who are always present
along the Suez Canal and at Sharm-el-Sheikh, we didn't see a
single soldier or policeman anywhere. The only official we
saw wasn't even Jewish. He was a young Mexican physician

who had volunteered to serve for a year or two in the Israeli Ministry of Health in order to look after the medical needs of the Bedouins. We met him at an oasis not far from the Santa Caterina Monastery, which is at the foot of Mount Sinai where the Lord gave Moses the tablets of the Ten Commandments.

In his book, *The Cursed Blessing: The Story of Israel's Occupation of the West Bank,* Shabtai Teveth personalizes the Israeli approach to the occupation by quoting this admonition by General Dayan to one of his military governors in 1967:

> Listen, Zonik, don't boss them. Leave them alone. Don't educate them and don't teach them [our ways and our culture]. With regard to security you have your orders. Go right ahead—a strong arm. You demolished a house from which shots were fired—so you demolished it. But as for the rest, leave them alone. What do you need all these barriers for? Let them move around freely, on foot and by car. Let them go to their fields, to their businesses. Don't rule them. And besides, why are there so many soldiers in the town? Get them out of town. Deploy the units in camps outside the town. What do you need the Army in the town for? You don't have to be seen. The city must appear as if it hasn't been occupied. Return the requisitioned equipment and vehicles to the people. See that it's done quickly and that everything is in good condition. Evacuate the area. Give them the feeling that the war is over and that nothing has changed. The Mayor runs the municipality as always. If there is need for intervention, we will act. The [Military] Governor will extend aid only if he is approached.

Earlier, Dayan had said to another general: "Don't make the same mistake that the Americans made in Vietnam. See to it that the essential services return to normal . . . but they must be run by the Arabs themselves. . . . Don't trouble to try and make the Arabs love you."

Dayan had used the same direct, straightforward language to the Arabs themselves, which is why even the bitterest enemies of Israel among them respect him. Quite early in the occupation of the West Bank, he told the Notables of Nablus, again according to Teveth:

> Look here, dear sirs, you lost the war and I don't know what's in store, another military confrontation or peace talks. For my part, I want peace, not war. But what is clear is that you . . . are powerless to do anything one way or another. In the interim period you have the option of either rebeling or of acquiescing in the situation. I expect the population and civilian institutions to carry on normally with their administrative functions, while we . . . will fulfill the governmental duties imposed on us. The choice you have is either orderly life or rebellion. But you should know that if you choose rebellion, we'll have no option but to break you.

By and large, while they may reject Israeli rule in their hearts and minds, the overwhelming number of Arabs in the most populated of the occupied areas—the West Bank, the Gaza Strip and East Jerusalem—have not violently resisted it with acts. Why?

First of all, Jordan and Egypt acquired the West Bank and the Gaza Strip respectively by conquest in the first Arab-Israel War of 1948, when they, together with other Arab states, sought to overturn the 1947 United Nations General Assembly resolution calling for separate Arab and Jewish states in what was then British Palestine. While they failed to destroy the infant Jewish State, they also failed to establish a Palestinian Arab State in the areas not taken by Israel. Instead, they treated the Arab Palestinians with disdain and contempt. Egypt didn't even allow them citizenship or freedom of movement out of the Gaza Strip. That is why many West Bankers and Gazans have no great love for King Hussein or President Sadat.

Second, within the limits of the continuing formal state of war (and a toothless terrorism within the territories themselves), Israeli rule has in fact been correct, efficient, humane, and benign. And the Palestinians know it, even if Radio Cairo and Radio Damascus profess that they do not. So much so that Cabinet member Moshe Kol, the Minister of Tourism, recently complained that Israeli-Arab citizens "are often subjected to more frustration than the Arabs living under military government in the areas."

Also, Defense Minister Dayan, partly because he is a restless man who hates to be tied down to desks and details, partly because he loves moving about outdoors, partly because he hates red tape—and Israeli red tape is among the world's worst—and partly because he respects the Arabs even as he must oppose them, makes it a regular practice to meet with their leaders in the territories. He listens quietly to their grievances and does something about them whenever he believes that they are justified. For instance, in June 1971 he visited the Gaza Strip and promised the Notables there that any member of the Israeli military and police who used unwarranted force while discharging his responsibilities would be court-martialed. There is even the interesting case on record of Jamil Hamad, the editor of a Bethlehem weekly, who, together with some other residents of that holy town, protested the suspension in July of 1971 of Lieutenant Colonel Yehoshua Ne'eman, the district Military Governor. Colonel Ne'eman was suspended because he allegedly mistreated a local Bethlehemite. But Mr. Hamad said at the time: "I myself am not keen on seeing Israel Military Governors around. But an officer who behaves in strict correctness must not be downgraded because of one man's complaint."

A third reason for the relative and continuing calm in the territories is the freedom of expression—in speech, in writing, in movement, in choice of trade or profession, and in non-violent politics (up to and including the recently held local elections)—which the Israeli military authorities allow the inhabitants. A free press was not common to the areas before the Israelis came to them. It is now. True, articles dealing with "security" must be submitted to the military censor prior to publication. But this is a stipulation that applies to *all* journalists, Israeli and foreign, Jew and Arab, resident of Israel proper or of the administered territories. Journalists in the territories can and do publish the most vitriolic material against the occupation. As long as it does not actually violate security, it is passed by the censor.

In the whole history of the Israeli State and of the Israeli occupation, there has been only one case of a working journalist, Arab or Jew, being arrested by the authorities because of what he wrote. That happened when the two editors of an Arab bi-weekly, who oppose both the West Bank Arab "Establishment" and the Jordanians as well, failed to submit to the censor an article they published after Israel's famous raid on El Fatah headquarters in Beirut in late Spring 1973. They charged "an Israeli-Jordanian conspiracy behind the Beirut raid." At the time, *M.I.S.*, a fortnightly Middle East intelligence survey published in Tel-Aviv, wrote: "On April 26 [1973], the editors were released on bail. The Israeli authorities, showing signs of embarrassment over the incident, made no public statements on whether charges would be pressed. No further action to check free expression in the Arab press appeared likely. After the initial shock of West Bank reaction to the raid subsided, the Israeli authorities concluded that the expressions of solidarity notwithstanding, West Bank society generally does not endorse the political program or the guerrilla strategy of the Fidayeen [terrorists]."

As for listening to foreign Arab radio and television stations, including the stations of the terrorists themselves, the Israelis allow the occupied Arabs to do so to their hearts' content. The broadcasts are never jammed and the Arabs can watch or hear them whenever and for as long as they wish. As far as the Military Government is concerned, it is anti-Israel *acts*—rioting, the harboring of terrorists, and terrorism itself—not anti-Israel *words* that determines the boundary between permissible and impermissible behavior. Words of hatred bring no Israeli reaction. Acts of resistance do. In the latter case, the response ranges from the blowing up of individual houses, to arrest and trial, to exile, usually to Jordan.

A fourth reason for Israeli success in the territories is their unique approach to civil disobedience, or passive resistance.

In the first two years of the occupation, civil disobedience was quite popular and frequent. Whenever the anniversaries of the Balfour Declaration (the 1917 British government statement viewing "with favor the establishment in Palestine of a national home for the Jewish people"), the 1947 UN Palestine partition resolution, the 1948 proclamation by the Jews of the State of Israel, the 1967 Six Day War came around, or on other *ad hoc* occasions, Arab schools and shops would close down and there would be demonstrations of various sorts. But instead of forcing the schools and shops to open and breaking the demonstrations à la Kent State University, the Israelis would simply say to the Arabs: "If you want to, keep your schools shut down. It will be your children who won't be educated and your teachers and administrators who won't get paid. The same thing goes for your shops, factories, and farms. The longer you keep them closed and unworked, the less money will be made by both employers and employees and the less you will all have to feed your families with."

As General Gazit said in an interview published in the *Jerusalem Post Weekly* of June 13, 1972:

> We refused to do what they wanted us to do—to send in soldiers and police with weapons and batons to beat up children and be photographed doing so. All we did was announce that there would be a curfew imposed immediately, and anybody outside would be shot. No shooting was ever necessary.

> At the beginning they got good publicity results. But there is a law of diminishing returns applying to publicity. . . . [Even] our own press got bored. So did the people—and they were the only sufferers from the closed shops and schools.

> The next thing we did was to exile their leaders. In all, only about seventy people were exiled. After all, this was not such a great punishment—we sent them to Amman, to their own people, to honour and comfort. This is not the same as imprisoning them, which would have made martyrs of them.

53

The ultimate result of this anti-civil disobedience posture is that there has been no overt non-cooperation with the Israelis, no boycotts, closings, and street demonstrations since September 1969.

The fifth Israeli instrument for quieting the territories is their successful campaign against armed terrorist resistance. They have been aided by the fact that Mao Tse-Tung's rules about the intimate relationship between insurgents and the people they are trying to "liberate" (in which the latter are the water and the former the fish) have never been able to take root in the Arab territories.

"How may it be," writes Mao, "that these two cannot exist together? It is only undisciplined troops [i.e., guerrillas] who make the people their enemies and who, like the fish out of its native element, cannot live." In this "fish and water" matter the Israelis have really been much luckier than they realize or care to admit. For one truly wonders how they would have fared if they had an enemy as dedicated, disciplined, trained, and patient as, let us say, the Vietcong or the North Vietnamese in Indochina or the Communists in Mainland China.

In any case, one deals with the enemy one has. And here the Israelis have been fortunate that their enemies do not, in the main, possess the qualities extolled by Chairman Mao for prosecuting protracted wars of national liberation. Except for an occasional incident here and there—and "there" increasingly means beyond the territories and of Israel herself, and in the alleyways or airports of Athens, London, Munich, Madrid, Paris, Rome, Beirut, Nicosia and elsewhere—terrorism is practically licked.

Part of this success is due to the existence of some twenty strategically located armed agricultural outposts staffed by special groups of men and women—the soldier-farmers of the Nahal branch of the Army. Nahal is an acronym composed from the Hebrew words Noar Halutzi Lochem (Fighting Pioneer Youth). Part of Israel's success is due to amazing counterintelligence by Israelis who look like Arabs and who speak Arabic in whatever dialect the mission requires. Part is due to quick

punishment, meaning imprisonment not death, whenever terrorists are caught. Part is due to a code of conduct which
compels the Israeli military to pay pensions to the dependents
of those who have fought against Israel. Prof. Yoram Dinstein,
in a piece he wrote for the August 4, 1972 issue of *The Israel
Digest,* makes much of this point:

> Possibly the most peculiar aspect of the Israeli occupa-
> tion is that all the liberal policies have been introduced by
> the military, unprodded, and at times only lukewarmly sup-
> ported, by the civilians. An interesting case . . . came to
> light at the recent Tel-Aviv International Symposium [on
> human rights]. The State Attorney, Mr. Gabriel Bach, . . .
> referred to the fact that Israel opted to introduce its ad-
> vanced social welfare system into the West Bank, and even
> paid pensions to widows and orphans whose fathers and
> husbands had died in battle against us in the Six Day War.
> That, Mr. Bach, said, he understood and accepted. But he
> had learned that the Military Government had also decided
> to give financial support to women whose husbands had left
> their families to join El Fatah. Was that not going a little
> too far, the State Attorney asked. Are we not giving these
> terrorists the peace of mind of knowing that their families
> will be cared for, "so that they can concentrate fully on
> planting mines and throwing bombs and shooting people in
> the back?" The response of General Shlomo Gazit, Coor-
> dinator . . . in the Areas—in plain language, the man in
> charge—was terse and to the point. "We must deal with
> saboteurs separately; but a saboteur's wife, son, or father
> is not a saboteur."

Continued Prof. Dinstein:

> I would venture to suggest that while such an exchange
> could possibly take place elsewhere, in all other countries
> that I can think of the roles of the soldier and the lawyer
> would have been reversed. The lawyer would brandish the
> banner of individual responsibility, while the soldier would
> insinuate that support of a humane policy is tantamount to

aiding and abetting the enemy. Only in Israel is it the soldier who gives the lawyer a lesson in ethics.

Add to the foregoing Military Government measures the Visitors Program, which has allowed as many as 150,000 Arabs a year, *from all parts of the Arab world,* to visit the cities, towns, and seaside resorts of Israel. They talk to Israelis and see what they are like and what they have accomplished as civilians and not as soldiers. Add also the Open Bridges Policy. This allows West Bank and Gaza Strip residents to sell their products in Israel and to cross over each day (but not to stay overnight) and work behind the Kav Hayarok (the Green Line), an Israeli expression for the pre-1967 borders of Israel.

Estimates vary as to how many Arabs make the daily crossing—30,000, 40,000, 50,000. The Military Governor of the West Bank, General Vardi, says that of the 122,000 Arabs in his jurisdiction who are in the labor force, one-third work in Israel. But what is vastly more significant than the actual number is the *fact* that thousands of Arabs work in Israel each day. Some even work as auto mechanics in Army camps and workshops. All "occupied" Arabs who work in Israel receive the same pay as Israeli workers in the same kind of work. If they come through the official government labor exchanges, they receive the protection of the Histadrut, Israel's powerful national labor federation, and are entitled to the same social services as Israelis who have always lived on this side of the Green Line.

Thus economics—putting money in Arab pockets through work, not charity—is the real secret weapon for Israel's successful control of the territories and their inhabitants. The economic profile of the administered areas in the last several years is nothing short of astonishing. From 1968 to 1971, for example, the annual real term per capita growth rate in the Gross National Product was nineteen percent. The increase each year in private consumption was ten percent. The annual growth in employment was twelve percent, so that there is now no unemployment. These figures are even more amazing when we compare them with comparable figures in some of the surrounding states. During the years in question Syria's and Lebanon's GNP rose by 2.5 percent, Egypt's by 1.4 percent, and Jordan's fell. In 1971, while Jordan's per capita GNP was $245, for the occupied West Bank, Gaza Strip, and Northern Sinai it was $330.

This daily migration of well-paid Arab workers, as well as the agricultural and other assistance—$27 million in 1972 and $37 million in 1973—that Israel has poured into the territories themselves, has obviously been economically and politically satisfying in one respect. However, in other respects it has posed some serious problems.

For one thing, there is an intense labor shortage in the territories, particularly in farming, domestic help, and the more menial jobs. As a result, Shimon Peres, Israel's Minister of both Communications and Transport, has unsuccessfully suggested that Israel "should place work orders in the West Bank rather than bring West Bank workers into Israel."

For another thing, the daily labor migration has caused more and more Israelis to look down upon and shun low prestige, low status work, which many of them now call "Arab work." Especially is this so among the Oriental Jews, that is, Jews who were born, or whose fathers were born, in Arab countries like Morocco, Tunisia, Algeria, and Iraq. And the better-educated western, or Ashkenazic, Jews are no more interested in doing "Arab work" than their Sephardic brethren. Such an attitude among Israelis threatens to undermine one of the principal ideological pillars of Zionism and of the state it created.

One of the main goals of Zionism was the "normalization" of Jewish life. Not only were Jews to live in Israel. Not only were they to be the numerical and cultural majority in a state of their own. They were also to engage in the full spectrum of human labor, from the most menial to the most respected, that one would expect to find in a "normal" sovereign state. And the fact is that, in addition to professors, writers, scientists, physicians, painters, and other intellectuals and professionals, modern Israel has her Jewish postal clerks, garbage collectors, plumbers, cab drivers, truckers, farmers, foundry workers, merchant seamen, shopkeepers, cleaning women, janitors, and, yes, even her pimps and prostitutes! In short, there is a growing possibility that the inverted economic pyramid of too many professionals and merchants at the top and too few skilled and unskilled workers at the bottom, that characterizes Diaspora Jewry outside of Israel, and that the Zionists, particularly, the Socialists among them, worked so hard to change, may re-emerge.

And if the inverted economic pyramid re-emerges, it will not be because of Arab conquest, because of armed-to-the-teeth hostile Arab armies on the borders, because of the loyal minority of Arab Christians, Moslems, and Druzes who have lived in Israel since her birth. It will be because of the erstwhile enemies of Israel who may still hate the state and the very thought of its continuing existence, but who nevertheless come to work in it each day, giving their labor if not their loyalty.

For generations and centuries Jews have been praying, hoping, working, and fighting for their return to Jerusalem, Jerusalem pure and undivided. "Next year in Jerusalem," says the Diaspora Jew at the end of the fast-day of *Yom Kippur*, the Day of Atonement, the holiest day in the Hebrew calendar. "If I forgot thee, O Jerusalem, may my right hand be forgotten," says the Old Testament. Yet the irony of ironies, the paradox of paradoxes, is that Arabs from the places captured and still held by the Israelis since the Six Day War are the ones who are literally building the apartments that house the thousands of Jews now returning from all over the world to their beloved Jerusalem!

This phenomenon is showing itself in other ways as well. For example, as a rule, Arabs are very good at learning foreign languages. They certainly learn them better and more quickly than the average Israeli sabra. But no one can learn a language overnight. That is why Israelis, as well as tourists who can speak Hebrew, sometimes get this kind of an answer in Arabic-accented English or French or German from a waiter or porter or bartender in an Israeli hotel: "I am sorry sir. I don't speak Hebrew. I am learning it now. May I be of service anyway?"

If we speak of ironies and paradoxes, then the greatest of them all is that it took soldiers and war to do what diplomats and peace could not do since Israel's creation: bring individual Arabs and Jews into contact with one another on a daily basis. This is the Israeli military's greatest contribution. This is Zahal's most hopeful achievement. For while ongoing peaceful contact between Jews and Arabs will not by itself guarantee the peace that has so far eluded them both, the absence of such contact may well guarantee the protected conflict that has embroiled them both.

5

Censorship, Detention, and Deportation

EXCEPT FOR THOSE professionally concerned with Middle Eastern matters—businessmen, diplomats, journalists, scholars, soldiers, and the like—very few people living outside of the region realize that the legal tie between Israel and the Arab countries is one of belligerency. The only diffrence between the famous Arab-Israel wars of 1948, 1956, 1967 and 1973, as well as the so-called "War of Attrition" in the Suez Canal area that ended in 1970, and the relatively quiet periods between and since them is that the wars aroused the world's attention and fears, and the quiet periods did not.

The actual legal facts are these. Not at her birth and not now have the Arab countries recognized Israel's right to exist in *any* part of what was once called Palestine. They rejected the 1947 United Nations Partition Resolution and assumed a war posture against the UN-recommended Jewish State as the latter was aborning. They have never retreated from that original posture, despite numerous military defeats and other setbacks. Whatever written agreements the Arabs have been forced to sign with the Israelis are truces and armistices of unknown duration. Under international law, they do not signify the end of a war and the beginning of a formal state of peace. Instead they merely recognize the temporary stoppage of armed hostilities between the two sides at war. Unfortunatly, even in a democracy such as Israel, a state of war brings with it some form of military censorship. This explains why the table of organization of the Israeli Ministry of Defense calls for a Mail and Censorship division, headed by a Chief Censor. His activities, as well as those of his subordinates, extend to the pre-publication perusal of the copy of resident journalists, both local and foreign, whose articles might in any way impinge on Israeli security matters as defined by the Israelis.

However, in common with their counterparts in other democracies, Israeli military censors—someone has called them the Blue Pencil Brigade—have their quirks, peculiarities, and downright contradictions. For example, resident journalists and story writers must submit their copy for clearance. But nothing prevents someone from, let us say, the Bonn, Paris, or London bureaus of the *New York Times,* or the Columbia Broadcasting System, from flying into Israel, gathering his facts, interviews, and impressions, leaving the country with his notes and tapes, and then doing his story in some non-Israeli location for his newspaper or TV station. And it is not rare for that same person, especially if he's prominent, to repeat this process at a later date without the inconvenience that military censorship imposes on his Israeli-based colleagues.

Or consider this situation. Whenever an Israeli officer or soldier dies in battle, his rank, full name, home town, and sometimes his picture, are published in the newspapers. Some time ago the authorities decided not to hide these tragic facts from the general public. Hiding them wouldn't have worked anyway. For Israel's size makes her more like a family than a state. The country and population are small. At any given time, literally everyone has a father, brother, son, daughter, husband, sister, nephew, niece, uncle, cousin, or friend in the service. Yet the Israeli military almost never allows the family name of living officers to appear in print when they are on active duty —even if all is quiet on all the fronts and in all the places in between.

Then there is the fascinating case of what I like to call "The Great Censorship Contradiction: Or A Funny Thing Happened On The Way From 1968 To 1971." A foreign scholar who specializes in the non-military uses, particularly the peaceful uses, of military forces came to Israel in 1968 to do research for a new book. For part of his stay in Israel he was designated an official guest of both the Ministry of Foreign Affairs and the Ministry of Defense. This entitled him to escort officers and a chauffeur-driven car. He was allowed to visit non-combat military installations in or near the major cities and towns. The Israelis even let him visit a fortified military agricultural colony in occupied Jordan, near the Dead Sea. He talked with the then Prime Minister Levi Eshkol. He interviewed scores of military officers and former military officers, taking notes all the time. No one asked to read the notes. No one asked him to sign any censorship or clearance agreement. He came. He went. He wrote. He published. And to the best of his knowledge, no one in Israel or in Zahal was unhappy with what he wrote. Quite the contrary.

But then came 1971. The same author returned to Israel to do another book. When he approached the appropriate branch of the Army Spokesman's Office for cooperation, the entire conversation between him and the officer in charge was monitored and taken down by a lady officer of Zahal. Moreover, he was told point blank that if he was not prepared to sign and abide by all of the provisions of the following censorship agreement, he would "get no cooperation from the I.D.F. and no statistics from them of any kind."

To: Army Spokesmen/Public Relations Department

In consideration of your granting to me or procuring

for me or permitting me to obtain information of a confidential nature, and in consideration of your help in the collection of essential material needed by me, I hereby undertake not to publish, circulate or disseminate, publicly or privately, directly or indirectly, the book on .... or any publication in any form, verbal, written or otherwise, on the above mentioned subject, or any promotional material with respect thereto, without first submitting the material prepared for publication, for your prior examination in accordance with procedures set forth below and before your consent in writing having first been obtained. Such material shall be submitted to you at [address] .... and shall be deemed to have been submitted only when receipt thereof is acknowledged by you in writing. You shall be entitled to examine such material for such length of time as may be adequate for your purposes, in your sole discretion. Your judgement with respect to the publication of such materials will be final and binding upon me, in your complete discretion, without limitation and regardless of reason or without reason. I agree that if you shall in your opinion have any reason to believe that this undertaking has been or will be broken by me in any way, you will be entitled, without derogating from any other remedy which may be available to you, to obtain, from any competent court of law, in Israel or abroad, an injunction restraining any such breach, and you will be entitled to recover from me the costs thereby incurred. At your election, I agree that you may also or instead be entitled to recover a judgment against me in any such court for agreed and liquidated damages, which are hereby stipulated by me to be reasonably computed as being .... Dollars, but no such judgment shall have the effect of releasing me in any way from my covenants herein contained.

After reading and rereading this amazing agreement, the writer refused to sign it. In vain did he argue that: (1) he didn't want and wouldn't use any "information of a confidential nature," (2) there was nothing in the agreement that put any time limit on how long he would have to wait for Zahal's permission to publish, (3) a journalist lives by the clock and could write an article tomorrow if today's is rejected or seriously blue-penciled, (4) a scholar, on the other hand, lives by the calendar and can't write a book every day, week, month, or year, (5) to agree to legal proceedings against him "in Israel or abroad," should Zahal feel that he had violated his undertaking, was preposterous, (6) to agree to pay for such legal proceedings was even more preposterous, and (7) why restrictions in 1971 when he had received restriction-free cooperation three years earlier.

The officer listened very politely to his arguments but he did not budge an inch. No signing, no cooperation, he said. The writer still refused to sign, even though he was told that others had signed without such fuss.

Perplexed, puzzled, and not a little frustrated, he left the office on Tel-Aviv's Itamar Ben-Ari Street wondering what had happened between 1968 and 1971. Had Zahal changed its policies? If so, why? Suddenly, he got the idea of asking for an appointment with the Army Spokesman himself, whose office is at the Israeli Pentagon. To his surprise, the Army Spokesman agreed to see him, and rather quickly too. To his greater surprise, the Spokesman, who is truly one of the busiest officers in the Israeli Army, spent more than two hours with him. He answered in detail a long list of questions the writer had brought along. He had no objection to his guest taking notes. He did not read or ask for a copy of the notes. There were no agreements of any kind mentioned or signed. And to top it off, the spokesman gave the interviewer a bucket-full of very useful printed and mimeographed information. So much for the bureaucratic inconsistency of the Army of Israel.

As for the daily operation of military censorship, it is rather low-key and flexible, considering the continuous confrontation that has embraced Israel during the first twenty-five years of her existence. Working journalists do not find the censors overbearing or oppressive. Indeed, they find them open to persuasive logic and generally quite committed to the task of finding and keeping the delicate balance between the informational needs of a functioning democracy and the security needs of a beleaguered state.

Not only that. No writer in Israel really expects or would want to be allowed to print information dealing with, let us say, the size, deployment, and efficiency of military units, mobilization codes and techniques, or the numbers and exact characteristics of Israeli weapons. The overwhelming majority of Israelis—writers and ordinary citizens alike—simply do not feel that the country's press, radio, and television are unfree because they must submit to some form of military censorship, a censorship which, after all, has been sanctioned by the Knesset. And this feeling of freedom is enhanced by the fact that in all the years the censors have been censoring (and as often as not they let the copy pass exactly as submitted), only one journalist has been jailed and sentenced. His name is Amos Keinan. In 1971 he was sentenced to thirty-five days of imprisonment for "attacking an officer and slandering the Army." But he did it while he was in uniform on reserve duty, when he supposedly knew that he was subject to military discipline and military law.

Nevertheless, when all is said and done, censorship is censorship and there is a certain degree of incompatibility between it and democracy. As the *Jerusalem Post Weekly,* a journal that is subject to Israeli military censorship every day, has wisely written: "The blue pencil itself is a dangerous weapon, even when wielded by a friend."

In addition to censorship, the Israeli military has been given the right to detain and/or deport people from both sides of the Green Line if it feels that they are responsible for violence, incitement to violence, espionage, etc. Ironically, much of the authority for administrative detention and deportation stems from the so-called Emergency Regulations which the British used against the Palestinian Jews when they were fighting for their independence from Great Britain. The Knesset has simply carried these British Emergency Regulations over into the Israeli legal system.

Defense Minister Dayan disclosed some details and figures about Arab detainees in June 1971, when he replied in the Knesset to a parliamentary question by Emile Habibi of the New Communists party. At that time Dayan announced that the total number of detainees had gone down from 1,131 (in May 1970) to 560. Breaking down the figures geographically, he said that in 1970 there were 509 detainees from the West Bank, 556 from the Gaza Strip, 32 from East Jerusalem, and 34 from "west of the Green Line" (as he chose to refer to pre-1967 Israel). For the same geographic areas, the 1971 figures were respectively 229, 303, fourteen, and fourteen. While it is generally Israel's policy to bring the detainees to trial, Dayan admitted that this is not always possible (and therefore not always done). The principal reason for administrative detention is preventive security. Twice a year, each detainee's file is checked. As a result, he may be let free, his detention may be lengthened or shortened, or he may be deported altogether.

On the matter of deportation, the "Law Report" column of the February 21, 1971 issue of the *Jerusalem Post* has a detailed account of how the Israeli High Court of Justice reacted to a petition brought against the Minister of Defense by Azmi Ibrahim Marar, an Arab deportee. The account tells us much about the practice of detention and deportation, the regulations on which these actions are based, and the attitude of the highest judicial body in Israel toward them and toward Zahal.

Marar was detained for quite some time under Regulation 111 (1) of the 1945 Emergency Regulations. It says: "A Military Commander may by order direct that any person shall be detained in such place of detention as may be specified by the Military Commander in the order." Later, the Minister of Defense ordered him deported to Jordan under Regulation 112. That Regulation states: "(1) The Minister of Defense shall have power to make an order, under his hand, for the deportation of any person from Israel. A person in respect of whom a deportation order has been made shall remain out of Israel so long as the order remains in force. . . . (8) Any advisory committee appointed under the principal Regulations may, if requested to do so by any person in respect of whom a deportation order has been made under this Regulation, consider and make recommendations to the government in respect of any such deportation order."

Having asked for an advisory committee, which confirmed the original deportation order, Marar then appealed to the Israeli High Court of Justice. His main argument was that since he was already in detention there was no need to deport him. The Court unanimously dismissed his arguments and ruled in favor of the Minister of Defense and the military authorities. That of course was a blow to Marar. But what concerns anyone interested in civil-military relations in Israel today is the reasoning of the justices, as related by Doris Lankin, the writer of the *Post's* "Law Report" column.

One judge, Justice Haim Cohn, argued that "the High Court of Justice did not, *nor did they have to,* know what considerations of security lay behind the decision to deport the petitioner instead of continuing to hold him in detention. Furthermore, it appeared from the decision of the advisory committee . . . that that committee had in fact been informed of all the security considerations. . . . *As far as the High Court was concerned, this closed the subject.*" (The italics throughout are mine.)

With respect to one of Marar's points that the Defense Minister had no right to deport him to Jordan without the latter's expressed willingness to take him, Justice Cohn said that the Minister's *"unfettered power* may not be restricted by way of judicial interpretation, and it is up to the legislature to give its attention to the fact that it may result in the imposition of the same draconic punishment as was imposed on the first murderer, Cain." But even if the Knesset did not attend to this matter, Justice Cohn said that "*it may be safely assumed* that the defense authorities of Israel would . . . carefully weigh up the question of which country to deport the person concerned. . . . " He especially doubted that they would deport a person to any country where he would be punished for his political views.

The second judge, Justice Yitzchak Kister, discussed in his concurring opinion the relationship between the Emergency Regulations and the Israeli Supreme Court. The Regulations "are exceptional, because while Israel law in general accords the court's powers of control and supervision over the way it is implemented, the Emergency Regulations, made by the [British] mandatory government at a time of emergency and retained by the Israeli legislature because of the security situation, restrict the court's powers of control." Somewhat contradictorily, he added: "This does not mean, however, that the security authorities are not in duty bound to act in accordance with the municipal law or that they are not responsible for their actions."

The third judge, Justice Moshe Etzioni, noted that "although he understood and appreciated several of the petitioner's arguments, *it was not within the competence of the High Court to consider them.* For the matter of examining the Minister of Defense's considerations for deporting a person is entrusted by Regulation 112 exclusively to the advisory committee, whether this be desirable or not."

If the above decision by Israel's highest tribunal is typical, its implications are overwhelming. For while the military can in theory be challenged in the civil courts, the challenge is worthless in practice whenever the military choses to base its actions on the overly broad Emergency Regulations. Even if Zahal rarely abuses this extraordinary discretion, its "unfettered power" is incompatible with the minimum standards of civilian control of the military which a true democracy demands.

Israel is a true democracy. The extraordinary power to censor, detain, and deport was given to the Army by the elected national legislature and not taken by the Army itself. But Israel will become a much truer democracy when her people and their government feel secure enough to function without the ubiquitous Emergency Regulations, when her Knesset and courts are able to fetter some of the power of the Army of Israel

6

Ex-Zahalniks:
What Happens to Them?

AT THE END of the chapter on "The Sanctification of Zahal" I quoted a comparison made by an Israeli between the respected young and dynamic leaders of the Israeli Army and the petrified oldsters who run the country politically. The comparison was patently unflattering to the older generation and not a little unfair. For when it comes to translating generalized sentiments of respect into a practical system of rewards, the men of yesterday, the party dogmatists, have treated former senior officers of the Army very well, very well indeed. They have done it by allowing—one may even say, enticing—them into the upper reaches of business, the civil bureaucracy, university teaching and administration, and (as we shall see in a later chapter) politics itself. The following random list of military retirees and the jobs they hold or have held at this writing easily proves the point.

General Meir Amit is the head of Koor, a labor union-owned conglomerate of more than thirty-five companies. It is perhaps

Israel's largest industrial complex. After defense, Israel's greatest need is immigration, called *aliyah* in Hebrew. It is therefore very much to the point that the director of the World Zionist Organization's Aliyah and Absorption Department is General Uzi Narkiss, the Liberator of Jerusalem's Old City. Colonel Mordechai M. Bar-On is the head of the World Zionist Organization's Youth and Hechalutz (Pioneer) Department.

Yad Vashem is the sadly beautiful building and archive that Israel constructed in Jerusalem to memorialize the millions of Jews the Nazis murdered in World War II. General Yitzchak Arad heads it. General Yosef Avidar is comptroller of the Histadrut—the largest labor union in the world, when one relates its membership to the total population of a country. General Haim Bar-Lev, after whom the famous "Bar-Lev Line" at the Suez Canal was named, joined the government as Minister of Commerce and Industry immediately upon retiring as Chief of Staff. Netanel Lorch, one-time head of the General Staff's History Branch was for several years the director of the Latin American Division of the Foreign Ministry. Ze'ev Bashan, a former lieutenant colonel, is Israel's first Ambassador to Haiti. And General Yitzchak Rabin, the Chief of Staff during the Six Day War, served for some five years in Israel's most important foreign diplomatic post—the Ambassador to the United States.

The list continues. Rabbi Shlomo Goren moved from Chief Army Chaplain to Chief Ashkenazic Rabbi of Tel-Aviv to Chief Ashkenazic Rabbi of all Israel. Colonel Meir Shamgar went from Judge Advocate-General of Zahal and Legal Advisor to the Ministry of Defense to the job of Attorney-General of Israel. The late General Ya'acov Dori was from 1951 until 1965, President of the Haifa Technion, Israel's M.I.T. From 1965 until 1969 he was Deputy Mayor and member of the Haifa City Council. The present head of the Technion is General Amos Horev. Zahal's ombudsman is ex-Chief of Staff General Haim Laskov, who also served as head of the country's Ports Authority. Another ex-Chief of Staff, Mordecai Makleff, was once head of the Citrus Marketing Board. The present Deputy Prime Minister and Minister of Education and Culture is former General Yigal Allon. His director-general in the Ministry is General Elad Pelled, a former deputy general manager of the Israel Electric Corporation. Former intelligence chief, General Yehoshafat Harkabi, teaches at The Hebrew University, as does Yigal Yadin, the internationally acclaimed archeologist. Yadin resigned as Israel's second Chief of Staff some twenty years ago at the ripe old age of thirty-five!

The general manager of Israel Railways is Yehuda Reshef, whose last Army assignment was as head of the operations section of the General Staff. The current director of the Ports Authority is General Aharon Remez. The managing director of the Dead Sea Chemical Works is Colonel Arieh Shachar.

Upon leaving the Air Force, Colonel Peleg Tamir became director-general of the Israel Manufacturers Association. Former intelligence chief Colonel Benjamin Gibli runs Shemen, a company very similar to Proctor and Gamble in America. General Yosef Geva is connected with Supersol, the big supermarket chain. Colonel Aharon Nachshon is with the Bet Shemesh Motor Works. General Dan Tolkovsky is managing director of the Discount Bank's Investment Corporation. General Haim Herzog is chairman of the board of Keter, the big publishing house. General Avraham Yaffe has for years headed Israel's Nature Conservation Authority. Colonel Shmuel Kislev is manager of Lod International Airport. Ex-Chief of Staff Zvi Zur served for more than three years as head of Mekorot, the Water Company, before assuming his present post as principal assistant to Defense Minister Moshe Dayan.

And of course one must mention General Dayan in this context. It is he who, as Chief of Staff in the 1950's, instituted Zahal's policy of early promotion and early retirement, whereby an officer goes up or he goes out. Dayan's career is the perfect example of his "double life" or "second sphere of life" concept that forces officers to prepare themselves educationally and emotionally for a second career. His special distinction is that he is the only Defense Minister in Israel's history who made his first career in the Army.

If we move from personalities to percentages, the impact

of ex-Zahalniks on civilian Israel is even more stark. Thanks to two scholars, Amos Perlmutter of Harvard University and Shevach Weiss of Haifa University, we have some comparative data over time. In his book *Military and Politics in Israel,* Perlmutter has occupational data for retired Zahal colonels and generals as of 1966. According to him, the positions and percentages were as follows: politics (4.4), the Ministry of Defense (5.2), the Ministry for Foreign Affairs (6.9), other government ministries (21.7), government corporations (12.2), local government, mostly as administrators (2.6), university administrators and faculty (5.2), private corporations (22.4), independents (he doesn't explain this category) (12.2), returnees to their kibbutz (5.2), and others (2.0).

Weiss, who very kindly furnished me with a preliminary version of his article published in Haifa University's *Rivaon Lemekhkar Khevrati (Social Research Quarterly),* categorizes his results somewhat differently from Perlmutter. But his material has the virtue of being the very latest available; he dealt with 1973. According to Weiss, 10.7 percent of the ex-colonels and generals he studied went into politics, twenty-four percent into the defense establishment, 6.6 percent were in the Foreign Ministry or on assignment abroad for other official agencies, 10.7 percent were in senior administrative positions in public institutions, government corporations, and government authorities, eight percent were university teachers and researchers, another eight percent were university administrators, and thirty-two percent were senior managers in Israeli business and industry.

Clearly, the influence of former military people in key segments of Israeli civilian society increased dramatically in the seven-year interval between Perlmutter's and Weiss' work. In between, Leo Heiman, writing in the *Jewish Digest* of August 1969, claimed that ex-military men ran forty percent of Israeli big business, eighty percent of all government-controlled corporations, and ninety percent of Israel's transportation system including civil aviation. And in its issue of October 17, 1969, *Time* claimed that "since the Six Day War, nearly 100 former generals and colonels have taken command positions in private or government-owned industry, banking, utilities, commerce and transportation. Often, they are recruited to executive suites a year or more before they pick up their first pension check, and can choose among a dozen offers."

What are the reasons for "military infiltration" into Israeli civil life? First of all, Israel's gerontological elite—the average age of the cabinet and of the political leadership is probably the highest of any in the world—is as proud of and as grateful to the Army and the men who lead it as are the younger people who serve in it. On this question there is no generation gap whatsoever. Second, as part of the continuing process of military professionalization and depoliticalization, as well as that of tying the officer corps to the civilians they protect and defend, there is the already noted fact of early military retirement. Perlmutter points out that of the seven Chiefs of Staff between the creation of the State in 1948 and the Six Day War in 1967 five were not yet forty years old when appointed. During that period, the average age of lieutenant-colonels was between thirty and thirty-five, of colonels between thirty-five and forty, and generals between forty and forty-four. Now the average age of the top brass is creeping up. The present Chief of Staff, General David Elazar, was forty-six when he assumed command. Nevertheless, most senior commanders are out of uniform by the time they reach forty-five.

On this matter of early retirement of senior commanders, General Yeshayahu Gavish, a former member of the General Staff and a former Officer Commanding Southern Command, made this interesting observation, as reported by Moshe Ben-Shaul in his book *Generals of Israel*:

Zahal is built on a young generation. I still have to see the man whose leaving Zahal can cause a disaster. The young generation are no less capable than ours, and they are certainly better trained. And, besides, if there is no movement in the senior ranks there is no chance that a young, fresh, wide-awake army will be available to serve the State.

Age is an important factor. If we have Generals of, say, from fifty-five to sixty years, we shall become conservative and we shall be cut off from the junior ranks, the new generation. There is always the problem of the spirit and not only of the substance. It is my duty to understand my company commander and my platoon commander; I must understand his language, his slang, his meaning. Otherwise there will be no possibility of our being able to carry out an assignment together. So far there is no great difference of age between me and my regimental commanders. I am forty and the average regimental commander is thirty. I can still remember from my own experience what a regimental commander is and so there is still the possibility of full understanding between us. Of course I don't feel old, but it is a good thing that the Army does not leave this matter to your judgment, for no man feels when he has aged. As a matter of fact that is the real trouble, that all Zahal Generals are still young. I shall be glad to stay on in the Army, but I think that the succession of the generations within it is vital.

From Gavish's observation and the whole thrust of Zahal's retirement policy, it is clear that Zahal's "old soldiers" are young enough and good enough for a second, post-Army, career. And most people in Israel, whose population is only about three million, are anxious for them to engage in a second career. Unlike many Americans, who resent and reject the injection of ex-generals, admirals, colonels, and Navy captains into the economic and managerial life of the country, Israelis welcome such a trend. Indeed it appears at times that many public and private institutions and enterprises scurry about the country to get "their" colonels and "their" generals.

Partly this is due to the latters' great prestige and to the "ruboff" that accrues to the firms, governmental bodies, and political parties that attract these colonels and generals to their bosoms. Partly this is due to Israel's need to maximize her work force. But it is mostly due to Zahal's reputation as a meritocracy. This is in marked contrast to non-military Israel, which is deeply afflicted with the disease of proteksia (influence, favoritism, nepotism, cronyism, or "pull").

Perlmutter has put it this way: "'The high requirements for efficiency and merit in Zahal naturally make Zahal's veterans a most desirable element in civic society. Zahal's graduates are achievement-oriented, and are pragmatic and experienced managers. The highly nepotistic Histadrut [the national labor federation] enterprises; the politically appointed senior civil servants; the government-dominated 'private' co-operatives; and the politically oriented kibbutzim, all compete for the politically 'neutral' and administration-oriented Z a h a l officers."

Defense Minister Moshe Dayan made this proteksia comparison between civilian Israel and military Israel in an interview reported in the *Jerusalem Post* in 1968. The questioner asked: "Rotation in command is a guiding principle of the Israel Defense Forces. From Chief of Staff to the chief of the General Staff branch, changes are made every two, three or—maximum—four years. Seeing that Zahal is the most efficient organization in the State, do you believe this principle should be extended to Israel's political and public spheres?" Dayan's reply was:

> First of all the term rotation is not quite correct. Rotation as I understand it means circling round until you're back where you started. In Zahal there is a ladder of promotion and then—out you go. This is not rotation. The timetable or duration of service you mentioned also calls for some amendment. In some ranks it is much more mechanical. The last Chief of Staff, Rav-Aluf [Lieutenant-General] Rabin, served four years. As far as I can remember, . . . I also served four or five years . . . But in the technical units service is certainly much longer, five, six, seven, eight years —I see nothing wrong with that: I think it would be a good thing if the State had more new blood in key positions. This should apply alike to senior and non-senior officialdom as well as in politics. I do not say it should be a copy of Zahal. I would not say this.

The interviewer continued: "The blood circulation, as you

call it, in senior [civilian] positions is certainly sluggish. And it also seems to me that many appointments, even to [civilian] technical posts, are political appointments. How in your opinion can we achieve competition for these positions by criteria of ability and not of birth certificates or party cards?" Dayan's delicately worded answer was:

> I don't know that the birth certificate has any meaning. If a party card influences appointments that should be made on grounds of technical competence then it is very bad. I have no doubt that key positions and job advancement should be determined by objective criteria of ability . . . I assume that in a State which has in general a high official standard . . . a person in charge of a Government Ministry —I am very careful not to mention names—will not replace a first class professional man in a key position by a less qualified man. There is no explanation. It just cannot be . . . So the answer to your question, should the criterion be a party key—of course not. It should be a professional one, the best man should get the job. How to achieve this —I think that it is a question of what a particular country is prepared—or not prepared—to accept.

General Dayan and others to the contrary, Zahal is not, nor can it be, as proteksia-free, and even as politics-free, as they would have us believe. When it comes to the future of officers who obviously can't "hack it," their rise up the promotion ladder is quickly aborted. This happened to Amos Ben-Gurion, the son of David Ben-Gurion, the country's Founding Father, the man most responsible for setting Zahal's tone and guiding principles. Amos could not rise above the rank of major and B.G. or "the Old Man," as the elder Ben-Gurion was affectionately called by his countrymen, did not intervene. Nor is there any evidence that his son ever asked him to. For Amos to have asked for intervention and for B.G. to have intervened would have violated the principle of an officer corps based on merit which Ben-Gurion laid down in the State's first year.

Obviously, if the Army must make a choice for promotion

or assignment to a particular post between a more qualified and a less qualified man, the more qualified man will be chosen —always. But if the choice is between two officers of equal competence and stature, then it is not unknown for the choice to be made on the basis of friendship, or the fact that the successful candidate has the same political, personal, or professional orientation as the man who chose him. When this happens, it is an example of what I call "qualified cronyism." Perhaps it is unavoidable in any organization run by human beings, even an organization as exalted and efficient as the Israeli Army. But when it happens, it *is* proteksia. It may well be good proteksia, workable proteksia, acceptable proteksia, meritorious proteksia, but proteksia nonetheless.

But let us return to what has happened to former senior officers re-entering the civilian world. In the decade immediately following Israel's independence in 1948, there was a tendency for some, but not many, officers to enter active party politics. Former Transport Minister Moshe Carmel, Defense Minister Moshe Dayan, Deputy Prime Minister and Minister of Education and Culture Yigal Allon, and Minister Without Portfolio Israel Galili, who is Prime Minister Golda Meir's closest political confidant, are present examples of men who took this route. Most others took the route that led them into the public sector, principally in the decade prior to the Six Day War.

Since 1967, the gravitational pull has been toward the private sector. For one thing, the public sector is becoming saturated. For another, Israel's economy was booming and ex-Zahalniks have skills—in planning, budgeting, management, and administration—that the private sector needs and wants. Additionally, Israeli Army officers, always quick to create, adapt, and to learn, do not usually fall victim to what in the Israeli political and business sectors can best be described by the phrase "There is nothing more conservative than an old pioneer." Also, as *Time* put it so well in its issue cited above, "Israel's Zionist founders scorned commerce and were more interested in agriculture and socialist ideology than in industry."

This explains why Israelis, in contrast to Jews elsewhere (who have different pressures on them and different motivations), excel in soldiering and farming rather than in business, commerce, and management.

The most authoritative article on the Army and management is "Military Officers and Business Leaders: An Israeli Study in Contrasts," published in the March-April 1968 issue of Columbia University's *Journal of World Business* by Prof. Matthew Radom of Rutgers University. Radom served as a visiting professor in the Haifa Technion's Department of Industrial and Management Engineering in 1966.

Radom quotes three top Israeli executives. The director of the Israel Productivity Institute said: "The quality of management in this country is not satisfactory. This is partly due to lack of adequate know-how . . . Israel managers are too concerned with survival to pay attention to long-term prospects, and are too accustomed to disregarding efficiency to stick their necks out for it in difficult times. Needless to say, in this respect they faithfully reflect the general climate of surfeit and nepotism, which has not basically changed. . . . " The head of the holding company for the Histadrut's economic enterprises said: "The years of prosperity, easy profits, a seller's market, and high prices have brought about management practices in which productivity, profits, work norms, and the balance sheet did not count." And the then Labor Minister asserted: "There are no bad workers; there are only poor managers."

If the situation described by the three is so bad, what do Zahal officers have that others don't? According to Radom, while only one-third of Israel's military leaders have a university education, as compared to two-thirds of the civilian managing directors of government, private, and labor union-owned enterprises, most of the latter majored in the humanities and liberal arts. Few had studied engineering or economics. None had done any graduate work in business administration. Only 243 of them ever attended the three-months course in advanced management given by the Israel Management Center in the resort town of Netanya. By contrast, "virtually every I.D.F.

officer has received a top-notch professional education, and the art of management has not been neglected in his studies. A fair number undertake M.B.A. studies in Israel and such officers may be found at the leading graduate schools of business in the U.S."

When we turn from schooling to doing, we find, says Radom, that while military leaders are "particularly effective in their planning both for long-range and short-range objectives, . . . business leaders do very little long-range planning." While Israeli officers are "superb" organizers, decentralizers, and writers of clear, up-to-date plans, manuals, tables of organization, etc.," in business, management manuals are virtually unknown," as are other tools of the management art like job descriptions, tables of organizations, charts, and so on. And the unwillingness and inability of Israeli civilian managers to delegate responsibility to capable people below them is as legendary as it is loathsome.

Leo Heiman makes some of the same points in a slightly different way. In his article in the August 1969 issue of the *Jewish Digest* he writes; "Ex-military managers . . . plan everything according to Army-style procedures. Tactical planning means immediate production and bigger sales; strategic planning spells long-term development, hard sell campaigns and contracts. . . . Intelligence is learning about the competition and its methods, countering possible recession and other temporary setbacks through diversification and redeployment of resources." Given import quotas, tariffs, currency instability, price competition, and the many other ills that Israel must contend with in the domestic and international economic arenas, anything that former Zahal officers can do to give her a leg up is not only appreciated but vital to the ultimate, non-military, security of the State.

But the involvement of ex-Zahalniks in business and industry, (as well as politics, as we shall see in a later chapter), is not without its problems.

Any officer can take off his uniform physically. Not every one can doff it psychologically. Not every former commander can operate comfortably, capably, in a civilian hierarchy that is so unlike the one he grew up with. The military art of commanding soldiers is really quite different from the civilian art of persuading workers, unions, stockholders, bankers, and consumers. In the military, command depends upon obedience, which is more or less compulsory. In civilian life, persuasion depends upon acceptance, which is more or less voluntary. Not every retired military leader can see and appreciate this difference. Even if he can, he may not be able, for any number of reasons peculiar to himself and his background, to put the difference into daily practice as he deals with his subordinates, their problems, their motivations, and their aspirations. After all, pulling everyone together to save the State from military destruction is not the same thing as getting everyone to do his level best for the greater glory and profit of The Company. One former senior colonel who is making lots of money for his company expressed it to me this way. "Not every former commander can forget that he is no longer a commander who can give an order and go away secure in the knowledge that it will be carried out."

The result is that not every former Chief of Staff, not every ex-colonel or general, has been a smashing managerial and fiscal success. Some of them, especially on their first new job, have been smashing failures because they were simply not able to adjust to their new careers, their new colleagues, their new subordinates (the workers), and their new circumstances.

Another problem about officers in business that may or may not intensify as time passes is the fact that some of them, in the words of another former officer I interviewed, "are being caught up in the great political and moral crisis which is engulfing the country." What he means is that some of the new captains of commerce and industry from the Army, no matter how managerially successful they are in their new occupations, are being infected with the same materialism, high living, and fringe-benefits-paid-by-the-company psychology that characterizes many of the non-military members of the upper middle and upper classes of Israeli society. Rather than bringing new, positive, values to their civilian jobs, at least some ex-Zahalniks, he believes, are absorbing old, negative values. Similarly, in October 1973, Major General Rehavam ("Ghandi") Ze'evi, now Chief of the General Staff Branch, publicly "disapproved," according to the *Jerusalem Post*, "of contacts between serving officers and economic or public bodies, believing that this could influence the relationship between the body concerned and the branch of the army commanded by the officer."

A third problem is the jealousy factor. It is related directly to the way that socio-economic mobility works in Israel. In Israel job and status advancement occurs only vertically, never horizontally. Israelis must choose their career ladder early and they stay on that ladder, climbing quickly, slowly, or not at all. Individuals go into scholarship, or politics, or the civil service, or the professions, or the regular Army, or private business, or what have you. And that is where they usually remain for the rest of their productive lives.

There is very little lateral transfer, very little movement back and forth, between these ladders. There is nothing in Israel that resembles the American practice of businessmen doing a stint of government service and then going back to industry, only to show up again in Washington at some future date. Israeli lawyers don't move back and forth between elective office, private law practice, appointive office, and private law practice again. Israeli professors don't make a career in the university, take leaves to be senior government officials, and then return to academia again. An academic stays in academia, a politician stays in full-time politics, a medical man tends to his patients, a businessman stays in business.

The *only* exception to this unwritten rule is made for the former Zahal officer of senior rank. While almost everyone else in Israel must climb up a vertically walled vocational ladder as best he or she can, the retired military man *alone* is permitted to make a horizontal jump to the rungs of another ladder. And when he makes that jump, it is, as we have already seen, to a rung at the top or quite close to the top.

In time, such a system can only engender jealousy and even

animosity among those who are passed over. The man who has faithfully toiled for the party in the hope of someday getting a safe seat in the Israeli Parliament, or even a place in the Cabinet, only to see it given to General-So-and-So; the civil servant who has risen to the rank of deputy director-general of a ministry only to see the director-general's slot go to an ex-soldier; the manager who has his heart set on becoming the chief executive of his firm, government corporation, or Histadrut-run enterprise only to see the job going to Colonel So-and-So—all of these people cannot fail to be affected by the shattering of their dreams. At the very least, it will eventually lead to a lowering of morale and to a lessening of motivation among the competent civilians of Israel.

At the moment, it is not socially acceptable for Israelis to discuss this matter in public, just as it was once not good form for them to criticize the housing and other benefits given to new immigrants at the expense of Israelis already in the country. But civilian men of ambition cannot be expected to exempt ex-Zahalniks forever from criticism on this score. This will become true especially if the country enters a period of peace, but not one so permanent or secure that the size and importance of the officer corps diminishes significantly. It is only a matter of time before "vertically locked-in" civilians will voice their increasing resentment at the "horizontally hopping" military retirees. In fact, the present taboo against doing so may have already begun to break down.

The May 15, 1973 issue of the *Jerusalem Post* carries a story of the retirement of Major-General Mordechai Hod as chief of the Air Force. It says: "He has apparently set his heart on Israel Aircraft Industries. As yet, no such post seems to be in the offing. . . . " The same issue carries another story headlined "No Job For Ex-Air Chief?." It says:

> The former Air Force Chief's hopes of getting a top job in Israel Aircraft Industries may encounter difficulties to judge from a remark by I.A.I.s top executive here Thursday.
>
> Al Schwimmer, director-general of the Industries, was

asked by visitors from the Foreign Press Association to comment on reports that ex-Air Force Chief Mordechai Hod wanted to become an I.A.I. executive.

"He said he wanted to become director-general or chairman of the board, but as far as I know, neither of those jobs is vacant," Mr. Schwimmer said.

Mr. Schwimmer left the impression with his audience that he did not find Aluf [Major-General] Hod's statements proper.

But while Al Schwimmer saved his job from General Hod, I.A.I.'s board chairman did not. For six months later the *Post* carried an article which began: "The resignation of Michael Firon as chairman of the board of Israel Aircraft Industries is expected to be announced at a board meeting tomorrow. . . . He is expected to be replaced by the former O.C. [Officer Commanding] Air Force, Aluf Mordechai Hod."

There is also the latent question of whether ex-officers will dominate the civil bureaucracy and private managerial elite in time. Perhaps that time has already come. Perhaps not. But thoughtful Israelis ought to think about it. When PORI, Public Opinion Research of Israel, Ltd., asked Israelis in April 1972, "Who in your opinion will run the country in a hundred years' time?," 31.4 percent said that they didn't know and twenty-six percent answered "politicians." But the 12.6 percent who answered "Army officers" were exceeded only by the 12.8 percent who answered "scientists."

Finally, at a conference on the military at the University of Chicago in 1966, Colonel Mordechai M. Bar-On, who was then Chief Education Officer of the Israel Defense Forces and who is now a high Zionist official made this statement: "The society *must* offer the discharged soldier *and particularly the discharged commander* employment in a position that will appear *appropriate to the expectations aroused in him* during his army service, and which fit the *new image of himself* which he has developed. *The inability of the society to do so may*

83

cause a disastrous accumulation of social and political explosive."

I know Colonel Bar-On personally and I doubt that my last point crossed his mind when he made these remarks. But I have italicized some of his words in order to stress that in certain contexts certain people may construe them very dangerously. No matter what image a military commander has of himself, no matter what aspirations are aroused in him, no matter how popular and proficient he may be as a military leader, a democratic society owes him nothing but its gratitude and a very comfortable pension. It may give him more, but it does not owe him more. To state or even imply that it does is to create a mentality that may indeed lead to the disastrous accumulation of social and political explosive that Colonel Bar-On was talking about.

7

The Economics of
National Defense

IT ISN'T EASY to understand the mysteries of the
Israeli economy. It works, but not even economists are quite
sure how. Given the always-present burdens of defense, immigration, absorption, and development, juggling the economic
priorities is like a six-footer trying to cover himself with a four-
foot blanket. Any way he moves it, some part of him is going
to remain uncovered.

As far as Israel's economic blanket is concerned, it has
always covered the Army fully. The trick, as Minister of
Communications and of Transport Shimon Peres has written,
is to produce a "defense system powerful enough to meet for-
seeable danger, yet sufficiently limited so as not to destroy
the national economy." This Israel has managed to do. Far
from being destroyed, the economy has prospered. And, as we
shall see later, Peres argues that this is due in no little measure
to the Army and its technological and industrial needs.

The statistics of the situation indicate that until recently, whatever Zahal wanted Zahal got. In 1951, for instance, the then Chief of Staff, General Yigal Yadin, wanted to hold training maneuvers involving over 100,000 men. According to Moshe Dayan's biographer, Shabtai Teveth, this "was about all the manpower available to Israel at that time." Despite the opposition of the Finance Minister, the business community, the professional economists, and the others who predicted Israel's economic "ruin," General Yadin got his way. The maneuvers were held and neither the Army nor the economy was ruined.

If one studies the percentage of the country's Gross National Product given over to defense for the past twenty years, one discovers that it has grown almost steadily, ranging from a low of about four percent in 1955 to a high of about twenty-five percent in 1971, with the big bulge coming after the Six Day War. The Yom Kippur War of October 1973 may have cost Israel over $7 billion, an amount almost equal to the country's Gross National Product. (Compare this to the approximately ten percent of the American GNP given to the Pentagon during the bloodiest and costliest days of the Vietnam War.) Israel's large increases resulted from the War of Attrition between her and Egypt after 1967 and, of course, the 1973 war. At one time she was spending more than $3.5 million a day on defense during this period. The increases also came from the need for fortifying lines and settlements and from the cost of sophisticated American aircraft and electronic gear, which because of American inflation has climbed astronomically.

The cost of fortifying the lines and settlements exceeded $476 million; that of buying American weapons came to $936 million. A plane which sold for a million dollars in 1970 cost Israel $5 million in 1972. Now experts are predicting that each American military aircraft a decade from now will cost her twenty million dollars! This is a tremendous fiscal burden for a small, underpopulated country to carry, especially one committed to eliminating socio-economic gaps among segments of its population. One of the principal reasons Israel carries it is that she usually *pays* in dollars for all the military equipment she receives from the United States. She usually does not get grants.

If we change our statistical focus from the defense percentage of the GNP to the defense percentage of the total government budget, what do we find? We find that the percentages for security before the Six Day War, from 1965/66, for example, are the following. In that year it was twenty-five percent. In 1966/67 it was twenty-seven percent. In 1967/68 it was thirty-five percent. In 1968/69 it was a bit over thirty-six percent. In 1969/70 it was almost forty-one percent. In 1970/71 it was a whopping forty-seven percent of the whole government budget! The latter fiscal year saw the end of the War of Attrition between Israel and Egypt, the birth of the Israeli "Black Panthers," and the realization by government and citizen alike that Israel would have to devote more of her time, energy, and money to pressing internal problems. This explains why the defense percentages began to take a downward turn. So that in 1971/72 it declined to a little over thirty-eight percent and in 1972/73 it was about thirty-one percent.

But a figure of thirty-one percent is still nearly one-third of the Israeli government's expenditures. Obviously lower than the previous forty-seven percent, it still represents a terrible strain on the average Israeli. He now contributes well over $480 a year toward the defense of his country. This is one of the highest, if not the highest, per capita defense expenditures in the world. By contrast, the American per capita outlay is $380, the Russian $270, the British and the German $105, the Japanese $30, and the Jordanian $70. Over thirty percent of the Israeli's personal income goes to defense. Because of defense, Israel has a huge foreign debt. Depending on how one interprets her current government budget, debt maintenance and repayment ranges from ten to twenty percent of that budget. Little wonder that in a June 1971 speech, Finance Minister Pinchas Sapir said that the foreign debt yoke carried by each Israeli would "pass the $3,000 mark," adding that "this is a per capita world record which we would willingly give up." In that same year he reported that "we are spending over eighty percent of our tax revenue on defense." And lest the average Israeli should dream of an immediate loosening of the military's grip on his income, the Finance Minister is on record as predicting in October of 1972 a defense outlay of ten billion dollars in the ensuing six years.

What does the Israeli man-in-the-street think of all this? How does he react? Faced with the everyday problems of life, he will on an individual basis sometimes grumble. Richard C. Gross of United Press International captured some of these grumbles in a story that appeared in the October 8, 1972 edition of the Philadelphia *Sunday Bulletin,* about two days before Finance Minister Sapir's prediction. Gross wrote from Jerusalem:

> The tax collector may bite in other countries. In Israel he chews.

> Visitors, amazed at the high number of new cars on the road, the expensive fashions displayed in new boutiques and the growing availability of luxury items, . . . ask how the Israelis manage.

> "We don't," Yossi Shani, of Tel-Aviv, said. "You're in bankruptcy before you start here. The wages are not so bad, but the taxes are terribly high. It's very difficult to make ends meet on what is left of earnings."

> Very often ends do not meet for Israelis, the highest-taxed people in the world because of the high cost of national defense.

> For example, more than half the cost of a new car is taxes. A telephone costs $140, mostly taxes, to install. A can of shaving cream, taxable because it is considered a luxury, costs $2.20.

> Just to get out of the country chews $145 out of the vacation budget for travel taxes. An Israeli cannot drive out because he is surrounded by Arab States.

Israelis complain that whatever is left after the initial income taxes get[s] gobbled up in the spiraling inflation. What cost the consumer $2.40 in 1969 costs him $3.12 now.

Buying a car can be a lifetime proposition for the average family. A small Ford, one that would cost $2,000 in Europe or the United States, carries a $5,000 price tag in Israel. Yet it is difficult to get a parking spot in Tel-Aviv.

Television sets, the crowded roofs in every neighborhood testifying to their abundance, run about $430 for the average model—nearly three times more than elsewhere—because they, too, are a luxury.

But before Israelis can even think c. buying these items, they have to survive the income tax.

"No matter how many hours a week I work, the government takes more and more taxes and I'm left with nothing," says Yigal Avraham, forty-two, of Netanya.

"I can't get ahead of myself. And it's not only me—it's all the working people. The big problem here for the working people is that you cannot live on your earnings."

As a result, a lot of Israelis live far beyond their means —on extended credit.

With most Israelis in a constant state of debt, most wives work, and people of both sexes look for after hours work, and many don't report this income to the tax collector.

Avraham is an office manager and a salesman in Tel-Aviv. He is married and has two teen-age children. Earning about $480 a month, he falls at the upper end of what the government considers to be the middle class among Israel's 900,000 tax-payers in a population of three million.

More than one-third of his salary—thirty-seven percent—

goes to the government, excluding social security and other payments.

More than forty percent of the tax money collected is officially earmarked for defense in a nation that has been in a constant state of war since 1948.

"We know we have to pay more because of defense, but when you are going to the grocer and to the butcher you can't tell him that," Avraham says. "He doesn't want to know about it because he has the same problem."

And yet, despite Gross's "slice-of-life" report—I have returned from my trips to Israel with the same kinds of reactions from individuals—whenever there are comprehensive national surveys, of *whole groups* of people, the reactions are different. Whether the difference is due to how one relates to a reporter who deals with attribution as compared to a researcher who deals with anonymity is unclear. What is clear is that despite gripes and grumbles, whenever Israelis are polled scientifically by professional survey researchers, such as the people who work for the Dahaf Research Institute or the already-mentioned Public Opinion Research Institute of Israel (PORI), they oppose reductions in the defense budget, reductions which obviously would lighten the personal economic woes of tax-payers like Yossi Shani and Yigal Avraham.

When Dahaf polled the public toward the end of 1971, fifty-six percent of those interviewed wanted the defense budget kept as it was, some twenty-four percent wanted it raised, and only a shade above nineteen percent wanted it lowered. Interestingly, it was those in the lower- and middle-income brackets, not those in the upper ones, who favored retaining or increasing the defense expenditure levels. The latter wanted them cut.

When PORI did the same thing as Dahaf, when during the week beginning October 28, 1971, it asked "Should or shouldn't there be a cut in the defense budget?," 21.1 percent said yes, 61.9 percent said no, sixteen percent didn't know, and 0.9 percent didn't answer. When, during the week beginning December 7, 1971, it asked the question "In your opinion does the Government spend too much, too little or just what is needed on defense?," it got the following aggregate responses. A shade over sixty-five percent answered "Just right," 12.5 percent answered "Too little," 8.6 percent answered "Too much," and the rest either didn't answer or said they didn't know. In the second PORI survey the responses according to income were somewhat different and more uniform than was the case with Dahaf's. In the "Just right" category, the percentages for those of above average, average, and below average incomes were respectively 66.5, 68.2, and 63.3. In the "Too little" category, they were 12.9, 13.4, and 10.7. In the "Too much" category, they were 9.2, 7.7, and again 9.2. In both surveys the strongest opposition to defense cutbacks came from people who were born in Israel.

Both the Dahaf and PORI surveys were conducted during the national debate over the 1972/73 government budget. As we have seen, that was the fiscal year that saw defense drop to a relatively low thirty-one percent as compared to the high forty-seven percent of two years earlier. It was a drop that was as strongly fought by the Defense Minister as it was defended by the Finance Minister. The final result was that the defense establishment did take a cut—a sizeable one—against its will, *for the first time in Israeli history*. Since the issue was hotly debated and well reported, a chronological discussion of it here would serve as a nice illustration of the factors and figures, as well as the reasoning, that ultimately affect the economics of national defense in Israel. (Unless otherwise indicated, much of the material for the discussion, including any direct quotations, comes from the *Jerusalem Post* or its weekly air mail edition.)

The Israeli fiscal year begins on April 1 of one calendar year and ends on March 31 of the next. This means that in order to have a budget covering the last nine months of 1972 and the first three of 1973, the Treasury officials had to begin to hammer it out in 1971. On October 25 of that year *Time* magazine reported that Finance Minister Sapir was demanding a sixteen percent reduction in defense expenditures and that Defense Minister Dayan was resisting the demand on the ground that he couldn't guarantee public safety. Both men, each of whom is a powerful contender for the Prime Minister's post after Golda Meir steps down, threatened to resign if they didn't get their way.

On November 8, the *New York Times* quoted Sapir as saying that "All the funds allocated for the purchase of Phantoms, Skyhawks, tanks, armored cars, electronic equipment and other purchases from abroad are sacrosanct." However, other items were not. They would have to be cut out or cut down. Reporting the views of the other side, the *Times* added: "Cutting back on military spending in favor of social welfare or improvement in living conditions faces the obvious argument that if Israel is not adequately defended against her more numerous Arab neighbors, there would eventually be little need for any other government services."

On November 16, General Dayan, it was reported, questioned the accuracy of saying that a quarter of the Israeli GNP was going to defense. His contention was that since contributions from the world-wide United Jewish Appeal and American governmental assistance had risen to some $600 million a year since the Six Day War, or about half of the annual defense total, the Israeli taxpayer probably wasn't paying out more than fifteen percent of the GNP for national security. That same taxpayer, he said, could not deny that general living standards had certainly gone up since the war. For some of them, the builders and buyers of the luxury apartments that were appearing like mushrooms, they had gone up quite a lot, "all in time of war. Was this the kind of situation which justified the non-purchase of tanks?," he asked, ignoring Finance Minister Sapir's promise a week before that his proposed cuts would not be at the expense of the "sacrosanct" purchase of tanks.

Also on November 16, Lea Ben-Dor, one of Israel's leading journalists, who served in the British Army during the Second

World War as part of the female Palestine Auxiliary Territorial Service, wrote:

> Just what is going on with the generals, the ex-generals, perhaps the Army? There is talk going around. The Army is extravagant and uses manpower even when there is no war, they waste food, my son saw it . . . There is a whispering campaign—more than that, long articles in an afternoon newspaper—that "the party" does not want to see so many generals in the government. There are only two generals in the government now, Yigal Allon, whose Army career ended in 1949, and Moshe Dayan, and most people want him. Those who perhaps feel they could do without him, especially as long as the prolonged cease-fire continues, are loud in his praises but find a lot of faults in an Army that is no longer silencing all criticism by winning battles and losing men.

> May the cease-fire last and the criticism continue. The budget cuts whose way is being smoothed by the criticism may affect Army efficiency, but the Army will presumably fight excessive cuts as it fights any other inroads into its operating capacity. The sad truth is that except in lives, a nonfighting army is little cheaper than a fighting body, for which nothing is thought too good.

Two weeks later, Prof. Dan Patinkin of The Hebrew University, Israel's leading academic economist, entered the fray on the side of the Treasury. One of those favoring drastic defense cuts, Patinkin disputed Dayan's claim that voluntary contributions, particularly from American Jewry, paid for much of Israel's rising defense spending. And if defense imports, he told a Hebrew University symposium, were calculated properly, the defense budget's percentage of the GNP would be not twenty-five percent (as Dayan and others have indicated) but thirty percent.

On the same day, November 30, on which Prof. Patinkin's comments were reported, Lea Ben-Dor, donned her battledress again and returned to the fiscal wars. Coming down heavily on the Army's side, she wrote:

. . . how can you cut defense substantially? In the Golan [Heights] or on the [Suez] Canal? In pilot training? Hebrew University professors have learnedly told us that we cannot afford to spend so much on defense. We cannot really afford to be defeated either, or to lose men as the result of faulty equipment or lack of equipment.

Mr. Sapir was sure that no member of the [Parliament's] Finance Committee he was addressing would be willing to see second shifts in schools back in order to have more money for defense. And yet we have lived with worse things than second shifts in schools in the past. We have lived with not enough to eat for a part of the population. On the subject of second shifts Mr. Sapir might take a poll of families that have one son in the Army, whose equipment is at stake, and a child in the second grade, who might tiresomely have to go to school in the afternoon.

By the beginning of 1972 the Defense and Finance Ministers hammered out (almost literally) an agreement between them. Dayan had sought $1.5 billion for the military; Sapir gave him $1.2 billion with a promise to release an additional $83 million against next year's budget.

The extremely important thing here is not the exact amount of the defense cut because not everything that actually goes for defense is nicely labelled as such in the budget. Pinchas Sapir's famously effective bookkeeping wizardry is also not terribly important in this case. What is important is that, unlike previous years in which the military portion of the budget was neither criticized nor cut, in this one it was both criticized and cut.

As Sapir told the Knesset when he presented the budget to the legislators: "I am convinced that the public debates in recent months about the desirable size of the Defense Budget will contribute to this tendency to save. The effect of the public debates was that people recognized the need for the Defense Budget to be scrutinized, like the budget of any other

Ministry, in the light of general budgetary limitations and the scale of priorities laid down by the government."

All that need be said about the original 1973/74 budget estimates (see Appendix 2) is that they were shot to shreds by the war which began in October 1973. Had there been no Yom Kippur War, they would have represented a compromise between Pinchas Sapir and Moshe Dayan, one which apparently was "a greater concession on the part of the Defense Ministry than the Treasury." Defense is still the greatest single item in the budget—as, indeed, it must be until permanent peace comes to the Jews and the Arabs. But the increased amount asked for, mostly for fantastically priced foreign fighter planes and their spare parts, was less than the national rise in wage and price inflation. Had war not broken out again, the amount of all categories of social expenditures would have exceeded the amount for defense for the first time in Israeli history.

8

The Israeli
Military-Industrial
Complex

IN THE UNITED STATES the words "military-industrial complex" often carry a dirty connotation. They are considered to be negative, nasty, and naughty words. Not so in Israel. People there don't actually use this expression to label the relationship between their military and their industrial establishments. But if they did, they would not connote it pejoratively.

Just as Israelis generally welcome the influence of individual ex-officers in industry, so do they welcome the Army's collective influence in this sphere. The public attitude is that the Army's contribution is good, is positive, and is certainly necessary. Zahal not only defends the country militarily, Israelis believe. It also upgrades it technically and industrially, doing more than its share to make Israel in time a sort of Sweden or

Switzerland—perhaps even someday the Japan—of the Middle East.

In any event, whatever their attitudes and labels, the Israelis do possess a powerful military-industrial complex. It is large and it is pervasive. In many ways—for example, the fact that the Defense Ministry itself owns and controls companies that produce weapons and aircraft—the military's intrusion into the industrial sector is greater in Israel than it is in the United States.

In the days of British rule, Palestinian Jews made some weapons during the pandemonious period of revolutionary insurgency between Jew and Arab, Jew and Englishman, Arab and Englishman, and even, on occasion, between Jew and Jew. But it was a small operation: small arms made in small quantities in small hideaways, which the British Mandatory authorities uncovered more than once.

When his Britannic Majesty's Palestinian Jewish subjects finally became independent Israelis in May 1948, they found themselves in an entirely new weapons situation. Their neighbors sent in armies, with tanks, airplanes, and cannons, in an effort to subdue the new Jewish State. The Jews won that war, as they have won all the others since. But insofar as that victory was due to machines, not men—and it was really the other way around, the will of men winning out over the weight of machines—the few obsolete weapons which the Israelis got, they got from the few foreign sources willing to sell them to them at outlandish and outrageous prices.

From the very first moment of the State's proclamation, Israel faced a nearly complete weapons embargo. Her purchasing agents scoured the world to buy a Czech rifle and mortar here, a German Messerschmitt there, a rundown American C-47 transport, P-51 Mustang, or B-17 Flying Fortress in this junkyard, or a British Spitfire in that one. Of necessity, the infant Israel Air Force had to establish its own facilities for rebuilding planes.

A more far-reaching result of Israel's first encounter with a weapons embargo was her decision to strive for arms self-sufficiency, lessening, so far as possible, her political and military dependence on the wishes and whims of foreign states. If the trauma of 1948 put Israel into the weapons business, the trauma of 1967 made that business an obsession with her. The trauma referred to is not the Six Day War, which she won, but the struggle to break General de Gaulle's embargo against shipping her the already paid-for Mirage aircraft, which she lost. But perhaps "le grand Charles" did Israel a great service for which Israeli historians and politicians may someday praise and honor him. For as an "internationally known weapons engineer" anonymously told William Beecher of the *New York Times* in 1971.:

> I think France did us a favor, in a way, when it clamped a total embargo on us. Until then we had a partnership with France on a wide range of weapons developments that resulted in a reluctance by the [Israeli] government to go it alone.

> But since the French embargo the government attitude has undergone a dramatic reversal. Before, when a new weapon was under consideration, officials asked how much more it might cost to do it here, interests rates and so forth. Now, although we're pressed for funds, the calculation is weighted wildly in favor of self-sufficiency. We don't want again to be faced with a political decision that suddenly turns off our major source of supply.

It is this consuming fear of being caught with her powder dry—or without any powder altogether—which drives Israel compulsively to design, develop, and manufacture locally an ever increasing proportion of her military requirements. It is an open question whether a small natural-resources-poor country can ever completely free itself from dependence on foreign sources of military supply. For planes and electronic gear, for instance, Israel must now rely heavily on the United States, as she once relied on France.

Incidentally, a memorandum of understanding was quietly signed on November 1, 1971 between the director of the Israeli Purchasing Mission in the United States and American officials. It seems to indicate American willingness to help Israel become more self-sufficient in major weapons production. According to reports in the press, America has "streamlined procedures" for providing technical assistance to the Israeli weapons manufacturing industry, particularly for making components rather than whole systems.

The advantages to Israel of building at home such items as diesel engine transmissions for a new tank she is working on, or nose-wheel steering mechanisms for a jet trainer she already produces and the Super Mirage fighter she is going to produce, or the JA79 engine that powers the American Phantom F-4 fighter-bomber, the backbone of the Israeli Air Force, are obvious. But what are the advantages to the United States?

For one thing, there is the hope that as Israel becomes less visibly dependent on the United States for armaments—and what is more visible than "secret" shipments from one country to another?—there would be less of an "outcry" from the Arab states each time such shipments are made. For another thing, a more sophisticated indigenous arms industry would, it is believed, "put Israel in a better position, through sales to other nations, to finance more of her own defense needs." Presumably this would also lessen her need for military credits from the United States, something which also angers the Arabs. In any case, be it with or without American aid, Israelis are determined to reach their goal of full arms self-efficiency. If they don't reach it, it will not be because they haven't tried their darndest.

Including the regular Army, reserve units, and other security forces, twenty-five percent of working Israelis work for the military in one way or the other. With an officially recorded total employed work force of 997,000 in 1971, that makes the number of people involved about 249,000. If we exclude employed Israelis who are not Jews, then the number is 226,000. Even if real peace were to come to the Middle East tomorrow, it is unlikely that these figures would decline drastically or quickly. Finance Minister Pinchas Sapir has said as much himself. The *Jerusalem Post* of March 23, 1971 reported his views as follows: "The Minister said that there are no grounds for thinking that peace will lead to the liquidation of the military industries, including the sizeable labor force employed in defense projects, because we will still have to guard the peace after it is achieved." The most optimistic estimate that I have been able to come by was given to me by Yosef Almogi, the Minister of Labor, who told me in an interview that should permanent peace come to Israel, "ten percent of the work force would have to be in military industry."

Manpower is only one element in the defense equation. There is money, which was discussed in the last chapter. There is what the professionals call R & D, Research and Development. There is production. There is "spillover," or the adaptation of military technology and products to civilian use. There is the legal, administrative, and managerial manner in which the above elements are meshed together. And then there are the philosophical pros and cons of having a large military-industrial complex in a democracy, including the question of Israeli arms sales abroad.

As far as research, development, and production are concerned, these are for all practical purposes in the hands of the Israeli government itself. That is to say, the "industrial" half of the "military-industrial complex" is, with an occasional exception like the Soltam Company which is a private firm jointly owned by the Histadrut's Koor and investors from Scandinavia, an integral part of the Defense Ministry. The legal position is made quite explicit in the *Israel Government Year Book*. It contains the tables of organization of all government ministries. In the table of organization of the Ministry of Defense we find the "Armament Development Authority" (which is also heavily engaged in research), the "Directorate of Procurement and Production," "Israel Aircraft Industry" (which has more employees than *any* other single company in Israel), and the "Military Industries."

In other words, the military absorbed the weapons industry, enlarged the airplane industry, started the electronics industry, and has its finger on nuclear research and development. It of course did all this with the approval of the Cabinets, the Legislature, and the people of Israel. As a result, it is the nation's largest employer, after the Histadrut and the civilian bureaucracy, and probably its biggest customer.

Let us look at some of these military agencies in detail, beginning with Rafael, the Hebrew acronym and popular nickname for the Armament Development Authority. Its importance, as well as that of science and technology generally, is symbolized by the fact that in the Defense Ministry's table of organization, Rafael's director is listed third behind the Ministry's director-general, preceded only by the chief scientist and deputy chief scientist of the defense establishment. The director of Rafael and the chief scientists are listed even before the Ministry's deputy director-general. From the viewpoint of public administration this ranking is not without significance.

Instead of publication and visibility, most of Rafael's personnel must face secrecy and anonymity. This is a hard condition for research scientists and engineers, who are often driven by the need for peer recognition in order to do their very best work. Nevertheless, Rafael seems to have no difficulty in attracting and holding some of the best brains in Israel, despite the pay and other limitations of government service. Its personnel have close ties to the world-famous Technion—the Israel Institute of Technology in Haifa, and some of them are part-time faculty members at the Technion. It has some of the country's most sophisticated and advanced research and development facilities and a budget to make good use of them. It does a great deal of interdisciplinary work, which appeals to many scientists. But most important of all is the security, as well as the scientific, challenge that is involved. When a Rafael member invents some counter to a Soviet weapon, he is very conscious that he has made a contribution to Israeli science and technology. But he is even more conscious that he has contributed to the survival of the State.

Generally speaking, Rafael concentrates on weapons systems that foreign manufacturers are unable or unwilling to supply to Israel, on those which other countries are not working on or are not working on fast enough to help Israel, and on counters to immediate special threats posed by Israel's neighbors and their weapons suppliers. Its projects include small computers, airplane armaments, communications and electronics systems, explosives, fuses, bombs, rocket propellents and engines, and certain missiles like the Gabriel sea-to-sea missile, which Rafael researched and did the initial development on. Another military agency, Israel Aircraft Industry, completed Gabriel's development and now produces it for the Navy and for export.

From time to time Rafael reveals civilian applications of its work and the people responsible for them. One of its most prolific inventors is Dr. Boaz Popper. One of his inventions is a "revolutionary" transmission reduction device which cuts transmission from any power source from hundreds of revolutions per minute down to as little as one RPM. It has only four moving parts, none of them delicate or fragile, and Popper claims it should last indefinitely. Though obviously developed for a military purpose, the Popper invention can be used for such things as the fine-tuning of radios and other civilian instruments, for reducing the speed of a drill at the bit without doing so at the motor, or for mixing paints and other chemicals at exact and precise speeds. Another Rafael worker, Avi Lowy, invented a military device one of whose civilian applications is the quick attaching and detaching of car radio antennas. (This is not as small a contribution to the average Israeli's pocketbook as one might imagine, for the stealing of automobile antennas which, like everything else in Israel, are expensive, is a popular outdoor sport. Some even believe it to be a major business.)

Another component of the military-industrial complex is the Military Industries division of the Defense Ministry. What Rafael successfully researches, the latter and, in some cases, Israel Aircraft Industry, is responsible for producing. Judging from available statistics, as well as from the Israeli-made weapons and parts unveiled at the Twenty-fifth Anniversary celebrations in 1973, both MI and IAI have been as eminently successful in their tasks as Rafael has been in its.

According to figures released in a May 1973 radio interview with Yitzchak Ironi, the Defense Ministry's director-general, Israel now produces sixty percent of her total defense needs. In light weapons and ammunition, the figure is ninty-five to one hundred percent. In electronic gear, it is seventy to eighty percent.

As we move from statistics to specific weaponry, we find that Israel is developing or making the following items, some of which have excited foreign observers and buyers alike. The list includes a barrage rocket said to be "more accurate than the captured Soviet weapon after which it was modeled," a 155mm self-propelled gun, a 30mm aircraft cannon, a 105mm tank cannon, a 106mm recoilless rifle, a 160mm mortar, the Uzi submachine gun, an anti-personnel radar, army field communications equipment produced by Tadiran, the electronics firm started by the Defense Ministry, a tank, the Reshef (Flash) missile boat, the Shafrir (Canopy) air-to-air missile, the Jordan ground-to-ground missile, and the Gabriel sea-to-sea missile. The Gabriel was developed after the Israeli destroyer *Eilat* was sunk by a Soviet-supplied sea-to-sea missile fired into the Mediterranean from inside Alexandria's harbor.

Besides a military jet trainer, which has been in production for a number of years, Israel is working feverishly on her Super Mirage fighter and produces and sells abroad two IAI-made civilian planes, the Arava (Wilderness) and the Commodore Jet 1123, or the Westwind, as it is called by Atlantic Aviation, its American distributor. The Arava is a STOL, or short-takeoff-and-landing, turboprop aircraft which carries twenty passengers or 2.5 tons of cargo. Its military-freight version, twenty of which the Mexicans and other Latin American countries have ordered, can, in the words of an Israeli newspaper, "carry a squad of fully equipped assault troops or parachute these men (or a loaded jeep or similar type of reconnaissance car). With slight modifications, the plane can also be converted into a counter-insurgency aircraft carrying rocket pods for strafing

103

and machine guns or even light cannon." The Commodore Jet, or Westwind, is a long-range ten-seater, which the United States Coast Guard is now testing for a possible total purchase of forty planes, and which such American firms as Litton Industries have already bought.

But the Israeli weapon that has drawn the most recent attention is the new Galil (Galilee) assault rifle. Its capabilities are truly staggering. It is light, weighing only nine pounds. It has a collapsible bipod and stock. It can fire regular 5.56mm bullets—the same as those used in the American M-16—*as well as* anti-tank rockets, anti-personnel rockets, two-inch mortars, and smoke or signal flares. It can be used with equal ease by either the left-handed or the right-handed soldier. It contains a bottle opener, wire clippers, a night sight, and a flash shield which also doubles as a universal socket for rifle grenades, blank cartridges, and a bayonet. Its bullets can be fired at the rate of 650 rounds per minute at an effective range of 600 yards and a maximum range of 1000 yards. The waste gases from its firing chamber clean the gun so thoroughly that it is virtually impervious to snow, water, dust, and mud. Of its 104 parts, the soldier has to occasionally remove annd clean only five of them. And it is cheaper than the $120 to $150 that the American taxpayer must pay for his G.I.'s M-16 rifle.

No wonder that the Galil has been called the world's best weapon in its class, that in tests conducted by the American Army it outperformed the M-16, the Russian AK-47, the Belgian FN, the Italian Beretta, and the Japanese Har-18.

But aside from its own characteristics as a fighting weapon of great versatility, the Galil represents an important symbolic contribution to Israel's goal of military self-sufficiency. For as the *New York Times* observed when the rifle was first unveiled to the public in April of 1973, "With the introduction of the Galil into regular service this year, the Israeli soldier will be completely outfitted with Israeli-produced equipment—from his bayonet to his boots."

The massive infusion of Soviet weaponry into the Middle East after the 1967 war, caused the Israelis to increase their local arms production as fast and as much as possible. By the middle of 1971 they were already producing four times the amount before the Six Day War. With increasing arms production has come increasing arms sales abroad. Despite the stir created in some American circles in September 1973 about such sales to El Salvador, Mexico, and other Central and South American countries, selling arms to Asia, Africa, Latin America, and even Europe is a carefully cultivated part of Israeli foreign and fiscal policy. The aim is to earn hard currency for the development of the country in general and for the payment of military imports in particular.

In 1966 such exports amounted to $25 million. In 1967 the figure rose to $31 million. In 1968 it was $33 million. In 1970 it became $50 million. In 1971 it was $65 million. That year saw the sales of one item alone—the Gabriel sea-to-sea missile—reach $38 million. The defense export figure for 1972 was $70 million. And for fiscal year 1973/1974 the Defense Ministry's chief economist predicted that it would exceed $100 million, or some ten percent of Israel's total industrial exports. By 1975, according to the prediction of the director-general of the Defense Ministry, Israel's military sales abroad will reach $150 million! If that prediction comes to pass, it would mean a sixfold increase in a decade. It would also mean that earnings from military exports would top what Israel now earns from citrus exports, one of thee mainstays of her present hard currency earning system.

Not only do the Israelis sell military products produced within their own borders. In some cases they manufacture them in other countries in cooperation with foreign governments or companies. For example, Tadiran, which sells to some twenty countries including the United States, has two electronics plants already in operation overseas and three in the planning stage. All five plants—each in a different country which Israel has so far declined to name other than to say that one is in Western Europe—are for the production of "military electronics." Each plant's technical supervision is the responsibility of Tadiran. By early March of 1973 the five

105

plants had already ordered $30 million of Israel-made equipment. Another example of Israeli cooperation with foreign partners is the aircraft overhaul and repair operation which Israel Aircraft Industry is establishing in Mexico.

If the export of arms can be considered a regrettable result of the intrusion of the Israeli Army into Israeli industry, two other results cannot. One is in the area of labor relations and the other in the area of production standards and quality control. One of the Army's greatest contributions to Israel's campaign for industrialization and a better competitive position in the battle being fought by many countries to increase their exports is that the military's exacting standards for the local products it buys are slowly rubbing off on industries and products having nothing whatever to do with Zahal. More and more commercial enterprises, following Zahal's example, are putting more money and effort into research, development, and quality control. This can only be to Israel's advantage.

As for labor relations, while there has occasionally been a two- or three-hour work stoppage by some civilians at an Army installation, and even a technicians' strike at Rafael (the weapons development branch), management and labor have by and large gotten on well in military-owned industries and in civilian-owned plants doing work for the military. Soltam, the already-mentioned private firm that produces Israel's new 155mm field gun, has never had a strike in its twenty-two-year history. It shares profits with its workers and looks after their individual needs as much as possible.

Within the civilian establishment of the Army itself, labor relations are among the best in strike-torn Israel. This is due in part, according to a story in the *Jerusalem Post,* to the joint committees that deal with problems as they arise. Each committee has three workers' representatives, three Defense Ministry officials, and a Defense Ministry chairman. It "examines all complaints concerning friction between management and workers, as well as disputes between the employees. Where the differences of attitude are too great to be settled by simple goodwill, the worker is usually asked to leave, after proper compensation is assured—even if the joint board found that it was the employee who was right. The smooth running of work in this essential branch of industry demands harmony, cooperation and goodwill."

Harmony, cooperation, and goodwill are also required in the rest of the Israeli economy—in the ports, in the civil service, in the building trades, in the health clinics and hospitals, and elsewhere. But unfortunately, this lesson from Zahal the country has yet to learn. Featherbedded Israel has one of the highest, if not the highest, records of strike days in proportion to total workforce in the world. So long as she maintains this record, she negates some of the economic benefits generated by Zahal's example of meeting deadlines and raising the quality of Israeli-made goods, especially for export.

I have mentioned the name of Cabinet member Shimon Perès several times in this book. He, more than any other active politician, is responsible for "the arming of Israel," which, not unnaturally, is the subtitle of his book, *David's Sling*. It was he whom Ben-Gurion commissioned to work out the arms agreements between West Germany and Israel and between France and Israel. It was his leadership that accomplished the commanding influence of the Defense Ministry in Israel's military-industrial complex. He holds strongly to the view that the development of a country's military industry brings direct benefits to other segments of its economy and society. As regards Israel specifically, he and the others who were or are responsible for her remarkable accomplishments in military technology believe in perfect faith that these accomplishments fueled Israel's equally remarkable achievements in other areas of her booming economy. And very likely, they are right.

9

Religion
and the Army

MILLIONS OF WORDS have been printed to define
and describe "Israel" and "Zionism." But stripped to the very
nakedness of meaning, Israel is simply the only independent
state in the world where the adherents of the Jewish faith are
in the numerical majority. And Zionism is simply the ideology
that postulates the historical, political, and religious reasons
why that sovereign Jewish majority must reside in the Land of
Israel and no place else on earth.

Since the connection between Jews, Judaism, and the Jewish State is organic and unbreakable, it follows (for those who
accept Israel's reason for being) that the Army of Israel is
composed almost totally of Jews. It follows, further, that that
Army is based on Judaic precepts, which influence it and are
in turn influenced by it, as both the Rabbis and the Army struggle to adjust to the fact that a fighting Jewish force exists for
the first time in 2,000 years.

There are of course non-Jews in Zahal, as there are non-

Jewish citizens of the Jewish State. Bedouins and non-Arab Christians serve on a voluntary basis. Moslems are not subject to the compulsory provisions of the Defense Service Law, and relatively few of them join the Army as volunteers. Supposedly, they are not drafted to avoid placing them in a position where they might have to kill neighboring Arabs who are literally their brothers, since so many of them have relatives living in the surrounding states. More probably, however, the real reason is that they are not yet fully trusted, even though they displayed no disloyalty to the Jewish State since it was founded in 1948. Nor did they betray it during its major military crises in 1956, 1967, and 1973.

The only non-Jewish citizens of Israel who serve regularly and (at their own insistence) compulsorily in the Army are the Circassians and the Druzes. The Druzes look and dress and speak like Arabs and most outsiders think that they are. But they are not. Their religious practices and principles are in the main secret and not in accord with the usual tenets of Islam. More relevant to our discussion, however, is the interesting history of their attachment to the Jewish State and their service in the Jewish Army.

Until Israel's establishment, most Druzes kept themselves out of the military picture. But some, particularly in the Mount Carmel region above Haifa, were always in sympathy with Zionism and the pre-state Jewish community in Palestine. They fought in the *Palmach,* the shock troops of the Jewish underground, and when, towards the end of their stay in Palestine, the British interned important Jews, one of the people they could not find was Haifa's Mayor Abba Khoushy. They could not find him because he was hidden away in a Druze village.

"But the true, forged-in-blood partnership with Israel," in the words of Ya'acov Friedler, who wrote a fascinating account of the Druzes and their problems in the March 26, 1971 issue of the *Jerusalem Post,* "came early in 1948." Fawzi el Kaukji, the Syrian leader of a "Liberation Army," appealed to the Druzes, both in Syria and Palestine, to join him in his war against the Jews. Despite the refusal of the "venerated" Druze leader Sultan El Atrash to fight with Kaukji because he considered the 1948 Palestine War "an Arab affair," the latter managed to get 1500 Syrian Druzes to follow him anyway. According to Friedler:

> The Syrian Druze force joined battle with the Haganah at Ramat Yochanan, in its drive on Haifa, in April 1948. After three days of heavy and bitter fighting, they were soundly defeated and thrown back. Following this test of strength, the Israeli Druze, who had been "sitting on the fence," a classic posture for a small minority, . . . sent a delegation to the defeated "Liberation Army" survivors, persuaded them to change flags, and adopt the Magen [Shield of] David. To save face, the latter explained their change of heart by the fact that they had come to "liberate" their Druze brethren, but found them quite free. Many Israeli Druze then volunteered for the Army and served with distinction in the Independence War, the defeated unit included.
>
> Since then the loyalty of the Israel Druze to the State has been tested and cemented in three wars, which have claimed ninety-three young Druze lives in the Army, where they serve in a special Minorities Unit, and in the Border Police, where they serve in regular units. The demonstration of their loyalty reached its zenith during the Six Day War, when the Minorities Unit called up some of its reservists, a call that was answered 120 percent.

Why the Israelis integrate the Druzes in the Border Police, which has the important and sometimes deadly task of keeping saboteurs and terrorists from Israel and the occupied territories, and segregate them within the Army itself has never been made clear. Nor is it clear why in 1971 *Ramzor* (Traffic Light), the youth organ of the ruling Labor Party, reported that Druzes, Circassians, and Moslems would no longer have to serve in the Minorities Unit, while in its 1973 accounts of Israel's Twenty-fifth Anniversary military parade the *Jerusalem Post* wrote: "Of the marching troops, it was the Minorities Unit which drew the biggest applause."

These are certainly contradictions, as are some other practices regarding minorities and the Army. For example, Bedouins have fought with the Israelis since 1948, some of them in the Palmach. Members of the El Heib tribe, which makes its camp near Rosh Pina in Northern Israel, were among the founding members of Zahal's Minorities Unit. The El Khejarat tribe has sent a particularly large number of its sons to the Army, the Border Police, and the regular police. Yet Bedouins are not drafted and Bedouin parents of fallen sons are not eligible to join *Yad Le'banim*, the organization which commemorates soldiers who have died in action. Druzes, on the other hand, are drafted, and parents of fallen Druze sons are active in Yad Le'banim. Yet both Druzes and Bedouins serve in the Minorities Unit. Some young Druzes do not like this, as they do not like the fact that the highest Army rank so far attained by a Druze officer is that of major. And many of them resent the fact that Arabs don't serve involuntarily, enjoying "only the State's privileges without its duties." As one Druze citizen put it to Friedler, "while we give three years of our lives to the Army, the Arab youths either establish an income or get a flying start in the universities."

But since the Army of Israel is principally an army of Jews, it is to the relationship between Zahal and Judaism that we ought now to return.

In general terms, the military rabbinate does what chaplains do in any army. For Moslems, for example, it makes special arrangements for observing the Ramadan fast month. For Jews, it furnishes permanent and mobile synagogues, with their appropriate paraphernalia and accouterments. It sees to it that *kashrut* (the Jewish dietary laws) are observed, training cooks especially for this purpose. It expounds Jewish Orthodox beliefs and rituals, even among secular soldiers, by such means as an annual Army Bible Quiz, three-day courses in its own theological seminary, the distribution of Bibles to all new recruits, the circulation of its religious monthly, *Machanayim* (Two Camps), a reference to Genesis 32:3, and the compilation of a uniform daily prayerbook, as well as one for the High

Holy Days, and the Passover observance. These prayerbooks endeavor to combine the "customs and liturgies of all communities." To the extent that they bind together Sephardic and Ashkenazic Jews in the Army, they help to reduce some of the differences and tensions between these two major Jewish subgroups in civilian Israel.

Since in Israel all matters of personal status—marriage, divorce, birth, death, religious affiliation, religious conversion, and so on—lie exclusively within the jurisdiction of each religion, the Chaplaincy deals with these matters as they affect soldiers and their families. It also continuously studies Judaism's holy texts to solve problems arising out of military service in general and combat and front line deployment in particular. One result of these studies was the decision that the wives of the sailors lost in the sinking of the destroyer *Eilat* and in the mysterious disappearance of the submarine *Dakar* were permitted to remarry if they wished.

The activities of the military rabbinate before, during, and just after the Six Day War, as described in the 1967/68 *Israel Government Year Book,* are of special poignancy:

> In the emergency, the . . . main tasks were to hearten troops by personal ministrations at the front, ensuring means of religious worship . . . at all times and in all places, handling questions of identification and burial of the dead, and any necessary settlement of the status of widows.

> A prayer-book, to be read before going into battle, was printed, and every combat officer and man given a copy; every man in the field had a Bible; *Machanayim,* the Chaplaincy journal, was published every second day and distributed on all fronts.

> The Chaplaincy drew up protective proclamations as to the Holy Places in the administered areas, including Mount Sinai itself. Inviolability and free access for all faiths were the watchword. . . . In the first stages, the Chaplaincy was responsible for the Western Wall, Rachel's Tomb near Bethle-

hem, the Cave of Machpelah [the burial place of the Hebrew
Patriarchs Abraham, Isaac, and Jacob, and of the Matriarchs
Sarah, Rebecca, and Leah] and the Tomb of Joseph the Just
in Hebron, and the Tomb of the Prophet Samuel near Jerusalem.

While the fighting went on, all the Chaplaincy's personnel
and equipment were pressed into service to sustain dietary
laws and to avoid the contamination of what might be ritually
banned in captured stocks.

Emergency halachic [Jewish religious] laws went into
instant effect on general mobilization: certain religious sanc-
tions were mitigated, so that the war effort might not be halted
on the Sabbath Day.

Whatever is positive, good, and integrative about the Israeli
Army's approach to Judaism is mostly the work of a single
individual, Rabbi Shlomo Goren. He was the Chief Chaplain
of Zahal for most of its existence and is now the Ashkenazic
Chief Rabbi of Israel. Rabbi (or if one prefers his other title,
Retired Major General) Goren is very probably the greatest
living authority on Jews in military uniform. His personal
accomplishments are many, his professional contributions in-
valuable.

As a warrior, he is a trained rifleman, machinegunner, and
paratrooper. As a Rabbinic scholar, he has written a number
of theological books, one when he was only seventeen years old.
He is the one who set the religious tone and established the
religious practices of Zahal, particularly the resolution of ap-
parent contradictions between Orthodox Judaism—Reform, Conservative, and Reconstructionist Judaism are not officially recognized in Israel—and the needs of national security.

Rabbi Goren always objected to two sets of Army regulations,one for the observant and the other for the non-observant
Jew. He was against divisions within the Army between Ashkenazim and Sephardim, and against separate prayer books and
customs which might have led to the provision of as many as

eleven different synagogues at each Army camp. He successfully fought off the early demands of some of his Orthodox Rabbinic colleagues and of the Religious parties for special units for Orthodox soldiers and/or separate quarters for them in military installations. His standard reply to these suggestions was: "We shall never create new ghettoes here!" One of the things that he is particularly proud of is that in the Army, unlike civilian Israel, there are no Sephardic and Askenazic chaplains. Rather a kind of Rabbinic melting pot exists, probably in favor of the Ashkenazim.

But let Rabbi Goren speak in his own words:

> In the Army, we succeeded in achieving something not yet achieved in the civilian sector—the creation of a unified society wherein all types of people, from the extreme left to the extreme right, can live together. Ultra-Orthodox soldiers and atheistic kibbuzniks can eat together, train together and fly together. We succeeded in keeping the [civilian] religious-secularist *kulturkampf* out of the Army, thanks in large measure to the approach of the various Defense Ministers, especially the first, David Ben-Gurion [who was himself a non-observant Jew.] The Army of the State of Israel must be a homogeneous body, with no internal barriers.
>
> . . . we have achieved *kashrut* in every unit, observance of Shabbat and festivals (apart from vital defense activities, where the Tora itself demands that we break the Shabbat) and the inculcation of some basic Jewish knowledge into every soldier. Zahal is probably the first Jewish army ever where religious laws form part of the military code, and their violation is punishable by Army discipline.

This is not to say that there are not Israeli non-believers who bitterly resent the personal restrictions placed on them by the religious regulations of the Army. After all, if one is personally non-observant, one does not take kindly to the fact that on Saturdays all Army PXs are shut down, there are no hot meals served, and smoking is not permitted in the common areas of the camp. Similarly, except in cases of absolute military necessity, the handling of money, the turning of electricity on or off, and the driving of vehicles is disallowed on the Jewish Sabbath. And obviously this rankles a lot of soldiers who believe that Jewish religious laws are a lot of hogwash.

It is to say, however, that Rabbi Goren is known for his ingenuity in interpreting Jewish Law. For example, because soldiers are usually the ones most affected by the day's events, he ruled that they may listen to the radio on Saturday. Though no one questions his religious commitment to Judaism, some ultra-Orthodox elements decry his willingness to be modern and flexible, to bring Jewish Law into the twentieth century, as it were. And this is why Israel was treated to an unusual spectacle at the last election for the Ashkenazic Chief Rabbi of the State. Many Rabbis opposed Goren bitterly, as they still do, and many secularists and non-believers life Defense Minister Moshe Dayan and Premier Golda Meir welcomed his elevation warmly.

The value of whatever positive steps the Army and Rabbi Goren took to dampen down the fires of conflict between the secularists and the religious in Israel has been diminished by the furor over exemptions from Army service for two groups of Jews. One group are the yeshiva bocherim, young men who spend their time studying Judaism's sacred texts in Talmudic seminaries, or yeshivot. The other group, which amounts to as much as forty percent of the women eligible for military service, are those Israeli girls who ask for, and almost automatically receive, permanent exemption from the compulsory draft.

To understand the conflict some background is necessary. First of all, the ruling Labor Alignment and its predecessor parties have never been able to garner enough seats in Parliament to rule alone. They have always depended upon the Religious Bloc to form a functioning coalition government. Second, coalition government means compromise politics. Many of the compromises have been more in the direction of the religious elements than the number of their Knesset members would ordinarily warrant. Third, until the Arab-Israel problem is permanently solved, no responsible Israeli really wants to unleash a bloody *kulturkampf* between the Secularists and the Religionists, both of whom have one thing in common—intractability. Fourth, as already mentioned, pacifism is not a Jewish religious tenet. There is nothing in the Torah or the Talmud that precludes religious boys and girls from bearing arms, and most of them do. So that what we are talking about is a minority of *datim* (religious Jews), although in the case of the girls, it is a very substantial minority. Fifth, there are Orthodox parents who in civilian life really do keep their unmarried female progeny segregated from men outside of the immediate family. They are therefore neither insincere nor inconsistent when they wish to do the same thing within the Army. And what better way is there to do this than to keep them out of the Army altogether? Sixth, there are girls who receive religious exemptions from the Army one day and are seen wearing bikinis on the beach the next. This is something no self-respecting Orthodox girl would do and no self-respecting Orthodox father would permit. Seventh, if one goes to the Army, one may very well not come back alive; but if one doesn't go, he or she is allowing someone else to do the fighting and dying. This does nothing to diminish the pain and suffering of parents, wives, and children whose secular men have been maimed or killed in battle. And last, since this is a controversy involving religion, emotion rules reason, as it usually does in conflicts between zealots.

On the matter of the Yeshiva students, many religious Jews and most secularists are unaware that their exemption from Army service is not at all a result of coalition politics and party expediency. Rather, according to Rabbi Goren in a 1973 newspaper interview, "it started with a decision by [Socialist Labor Premier] David Ben-Gurion in 1947. . . . He told me the generation of Talmud students wiped out by the Germans during the Holocaust must be replaced. Although our defense forces were terribly short of men in those days, Ben-Gurion insisted on this deferment." Since in Rabbi Goren's view and that of others, the "lost generation" of Torah and Talmud scholars has not yet been replaced, present-day Israelis who devote themselves to this sacred task must be freed from serving in Zahal.

The issue has crossed party lines—neither the secular nor religious parties in Israel are monolithic—and produced some strange political bedfellows. The Independent Liberal Party has always been against the exemptions. Yet Defense Minister Moshe Dayan, a confirmed secularist, doesn't seem to mind them. When Gideon Hausner of the Independent Liberals asked a parliamentary question about the yeshiva deferments, Dayan replied that only about 6800 students are involved and that the yearly overall increase is only about 350. On the other hand, some members of the N.R.P., the National Religious Party, particularly those who live in religious kibbutzim, want to do away with yeshiva student exemptions. They forced through a resolution to that effect at the party's convention in March 1973. But it was rescinded the next day in the face of the opposition of Chief Rabbi Goren and his Sephardic colleague, Chief Rabbi Ovadyia Yosef, and the argument of one N.R.P. member that "even the Defense Minister had not dared to make this demand of us." And when, in 1972, Rabbi Goren was subject to harassment for the decision he handed down in the so-called Langer bastardy case, Prime Minister Golda Meir lashed out against yeshiva students who were doing much of the harassing. In a Cabinet statement of unheard-of bluntness she said:

> It seems to me that young men (like the ones who tried to assault the Chief Rabbi last week) were not exempted from Army service in order to be free to fight their own battles. Why should these young men be free so that they can intimidate Rabbi Goren? The yeshivot exist for the sake of studying Tora, and not to make it possible for young men to roam the streets assaulting people. These young men would be wise to realize that they cannot act as they fancy as though there were no government in Israel. I hope this behaviour will stop. But if the hooliganism continues, we shall have to discuss the question [of Army exemptions] particularly in those yeshivot

whose students will be found to have participated in this behavior.

The Prime Minister's threat prompted the *Jerusalem Post* to write: "Although violence has been endemic in certain yeshivot over controversial issues like autopsies, Sabbath transport, and missionary activity, an official warning that the privilege of Army exemption might be ended has no precedent. . . . " In turn, Rabbi Menachem Porush, a particularly fiery member of Parliament, angrily resented attempts by "secular persons to dictate in matters of *halacha* [Jewish religious law]," warning that if they persisted they would be responsible for a situation "which may lead to separation of religion and state and turn us into two nations."

Some time later, Leonard Perlov, a new American immigrant to Beersheba, who has two Army-eligible children, a boy and a girl, sent this letter which was published in the *Post*:

> There is a basic injustice in a system which allows certain elements of our population to evade their responsibilities to their country's defense by virtue of their religious practices. In this case, however, they claim special privileges by raising the cry of "status quo" instead of "halacha." "Status quo" justifies exempting yeshiva students from army service, and keeps their girls safely at home, while other people's children defend our borders.

> Some of these very same persons supported the resolution at the N.R.P. convention calling for their party's withdrawal from the government if certain territories are returned to Arab rule as a result of the bargaining which will take place when peace negotiations start. To me it seems a case of unmitigated gall that those who choose to keep their children from serving in Israel's defense should attempt to influence the government toward a policy which could easily delay the peace for years to come, thereby necessitating further sacrifices by those who serve in its defense.

In addition to the views of individual Israelis—be they

private citizens like Leonard Perlov or government officials like Prime Minister Meir and Tourism Minister Moshe Kol, who also opposes the present policy toward yeshiva students—there is some survey data about how the Israeli men and women in the street feel about this issue.

In August 1972, PORI polled a sample of the Israeli population on this question: "What is your opinion about enlisting yeshivot students; should they serve as any other young man, enlist for a short period only, or not serve at all?" The answers were revealing. A mite short of 82 percent said that they should serve as all other young men, approximately eleven percent said they should serve for a short time, two percent didn't answer, two percent didn't know what their opinion was, and only some 3.5 percent agreed that they shouldn't serve at all. Despite this overwhelming statistical evidence, the following month the government (which, remember, is a coalition between Labor and the Religious Bloc) decided to continue the policy of yeshiva student exemptions. The policy remains in effect to this day, even though it does not enjoy the support of the general public.

The issue of exempting those religious girls who want exemptions both from the Army and from alternative forms of civilian national service is even more emotional—on both sides. Partly this is due to the fact that Women's Lib has not yet come to Israel. Partly it is due to the honest desire of some Orthodox parents to keep their daughters home in a semi-cloistered atmosphere until they are married. Partly it is due to the known fact that while many truly religious girls gladly serve in Zahal, others who aren't observant at all don the cloak of religiosity to evade the draft. And partly it is due to the practice of some religious parents to refuse to let their girls go to the Army, but who send these same daughters to universities away from home, let them vacation abroad without chaperons, or work in civilian offices and attend parties at night with unattached men. (In fairness to the National Religious Party, however, it must be said that such practices are not sanctioned by the party. Dr. Yehuda Ben-Meir, a N.R.P. Knesset member, said as much when he told the Parliament: "These girls and their parents have no right to invoke religion to evade service in hospitals or schools.")

The emotional dimensions of the problem from the women's viewpoint are nicely summarized by two girls—one religious and the other not—who served in the Army. The first is Lieutenant Ora Mor, who comes from a religious kibbutz where all the female members have served in the Women's Army, or *Chen*. In the February 1971 issue of *Israel Magazine* she is quoted as saying: "It is not very ethical to make a cats-paw of religion. There is nothing in the Bible to keep people from joining the army. On the contrary, the Scriptures say that, in a war for survival, *everyone* must go out to fight—'the groom from his chamber and the bride from under her canopy.'" Lieutenant Mor admits that any Orthodox girl can go astray when she leaves her parents' home, but if she does, it's not because she joins the Army but because her faith is shallow. The girl who "is really strong in her religion remains just as strong in the army—perhaps even stronger, because she has to argue so much with the others that her convictions become deeper. There is absolutely nothing in army life," she says, "to stop you from being religious: the food is strictly kosher, you get your own two sets of dishes, and on Fridays you are allowed to leave for home earlier than the others, before the Sabbath falls. Draft-dodgers have no convincing arguments—only private reasons." And as for the matter that worries some religious parents the most—boys—she says: "Their behavior depends entirely on the girls."

The second female "witness" is Ziviah Ben-Shalom, a journalist and a confirmed secularist. As quoted in the March 1972 issue of the *Jewish Frontier*, the official organ of the Labor Zionist Alliance in the United States, she has written with some bitterness and irony:

The exemption of religious girls from the draft insults the army. What happens within its tents that may corrupt a decent Jewish daughter? Presumably, it is a place of wild orgies, co-ed sleeping quarters and bathrooms . . . [The] drafted girl is undressed and made to do a "kozatzka" in the officers' dining room. Or she is forced to engage in mass-orgies. That's what goes on in the Israeli Army. Don't you know that? Where have you been? I don't want to deal with the insult to the army—let the Minister of Defense worry about that! But I need not be silent about the insult to myself. If I wanted to create a scandal, and to become famous, I would bring suit against those who make certain announcements by which they are saying that I am not worthy of establishing a Jewish home and family. They imply that I am irresponsible because during twenty-four months, I wore khaki clothes. . . .

Continuing, she wrote:

Not only the women are being insulted—not merely those who have served in the army, are serving, and are being mobilized for service—but also their parents who are ready to surrender their daughters; and also the men who are later prepared to marry them and establish Jewish homes and families.

Finally, she asks the anti-military-service-for-women Orthodox zealots:

Is this your opinion of our daughters? Do you value their character and morality so lightly? Place so little confidence in their education? Are you so quick to disgrace their parents who raised them to pursue "mitzvot" [good deeds] and decent behavior? You are not ready to give her your confidence; to be sure that she will observe the Sabbath in a worldly society. . . . But if she is emotionally ready to have pre-marital relationships with a man, she will do so in civilian life. . . .

Even when the government overlooks the law *requiring* religiously exempted girls to do their national service, usually near their homes, in hospitals, schools, and welfare institutions —and the Government has overlooked it for over twenty years— and tries instead to get them to *volunteer* for non-military service, it faces the outraged cries of the ultra-Orthodox. And when this happens, the Socialist-dominated government always backs down.

Thus when, in 1971, Health Minister Victor Shemtov and Welfare Minister Michael Chazani sought to implement a nationwide campaign for such volunteering, the following examples of holy hell broke loose: (1) Rabbi Avraham Werdiger, a member of the Knesset Public Services Committee, said that not only would it be impossible for any power in Israel to draft Orthodox girls, but "a volunteer system wouldn't get them out of their homes either." (2) The Rabbinical Supreme Court of Israel brought an action against Minister Chazani, who is himself an N.R.P. member, on the grounds that in supporting national service for Orthodox girls he violated Jewish Law. This almost precipitated a constitutional crisis since the Rabbis claimed that their jurisdiction embraced every Jew, including a government minister, who violated halacha. (3) Fifty-nine Sephardic Rabbis placed large advertisements in several newspapers warning "We will not bow to this evil decree," and other extremists went to the Wailing Wall, Judaism's holiest shrine, sounded the ram's horn and beseeched "Our Father, Our King, repeal the evil sentence." (4) Mrs. Rachel Neriya, wife of a National Religious Party Knesset member and director of the government's program to encourage religious girls to opt for non-military national service, was forced to resign her post because of threats from young Orthodox zealots. One of their threats was to ignite a jeep full of explosives in front of her home. (5) Later, during the summer of 1973, her husband, Rabbi Moshe Neriya, submitted a bill to the Knesset calling for the end of military service for women altogether.

In this issue, as in the one concerning exemptions for men who are full-time yeshiva students, the Orthodox community in Israel is far from united. While some N.R.P. members fight the military draft and its alternatives tooth and nail, other members of the same party with, presumably, the same religious purity do not. Two of them even suggested publicly that voluntary service would be both good and workable because many of the religious girls "feel uncomfortable at the fact that other girls are doing national service while they are not." B'nei Akiva, the youth organization of the N.R.P., has actually expelled women who have dodged the draft on religious grounds. Religious collective settlements, such as the one Lieutenant Ora Mor comes from, have always urged their women to enlist. And Bar-Ilan, an Orthodox university located in Ramat Gan, offered free tuition (which is very high in Israel) to any religious girl who would volunteer for social service in lieu of military service.

Despite this lack of consensus within Orthodox circles, the Cabinet formally decided in August 1973 not to enforce the law regarding alternative forms of service for religious girls not going to the Army. This decision was taken with an eye to the national elections scheduled for the end of that year. Nevertheless, when the previously mentioned survey organization, PORI, polled the population on the question "What is your opinion on religious girls' enlistment; are you for enlisting religious girls for regular Army service, against Army service but for National Civil service, or do you think a religious girl should not leave her home at all?," it got the following results. Fifty-two percent were for regular Army service, almost thirty percent were for alternative civil service—a total of eighty-two percent—four percent had no opinion, 0.3 percent didn't answer, and only fourteen percent opposed any kind of service for religious girls. The figures for the females who were surveyed were pretty much the same: 52.7 percent for regular Army service, 26.8 percent for the other kinds of service, four percent had no opinion, 0.5 percent didn't answer, and sixteen percent wanted religious girls to stay at home.

If the PORI survey is accurate, it makes one thing crystal-clear. Whatever the political considerations that compelled certain members of the coalition Cabinet to vote as they did, these considerations did not conform to the wishes of the over-whelming majority of Israel's citizens, her women included. Not only that. At least half of the country's population are Sephardim. Many Sephardic girls from disadvantaged families from the Arab countries are Orthodox. They are given few

123

opportunities to broaden their educational and other horizons. National service, particularly in the Army, would do much to integrate them into Israeli society and culture. As Dr. Gerda Barag, a female psychiatrist from Tel-Aviv, put it in the same *Israel Magazine* article that quoted Lieutenant Ora Mor:

> The Army is very useful for girls who come from home atmospheres ranging rrom medieval to ultra-modern, from the polished uppercrust to classes where knives and forks are dear at any price. Here is a chance to even off, to fill in the gaps and cut things down to size, and frequently the parents themselves rely on the Army to make good the educational tasks in which they have failed. Of course, we don't know how permanent these changes are, but at least the girls gain a store of experiences which are different and often better than their home ruts, and which they might never have gotten otherwise.

There is one other thing we don't know: how many religious girls from every segment of religious Orthodoxy would dearly love to get out of their home ruts through Army or other service but can't—because of the expediency of coalition politics and the absence of any meaningful separation of Synagogue and State in modern Israel.

10

The Army in Education
and Social Integration

THE HIGHEST FORM of personal commitment for
a Diaspora Jew who calls himself a Zionist is emigrating to
Israel. And Israel's highest national purpose, after her physical
and economic survival is the "Ingathering of the Exiles."

Except for those Jews whose families have lived in Palestine-
Israel for countless generations, every Israeli is an immigrant—
or the child, grandchild, or great-grandchild of one. Thus
absorbing immigrants into the social body of the State is a
supreme duty, which all government agencies share, including
the Army. If defending the State is Zahal's primary task, integrating its citizens—both old and new—is its main secondary
task.

David Ben-Gurion decreed it so. In 1949 he declared that
it "is the duty of the army to educate a pioneer generation,
healthy in body and spirit, courageous and loyal, which will
unite the broken tribes and diasporas to prepare itself to fulfill the historical tasks of the State of Israel through self-realiza-

125

tion." Chief of Staff General Yitzchak Rabin acknowledged this duty some twenty years later when, upon receiving an honorary Ph.D. from The Hebrew University, he said:

The world has recognized that the Israel Army is different from other armies. Although its first task is the military one of maintaining security, it has numerous peace-time roles, not of destruction but of construction and of strengthening the nation's cultural and moral resources.

Our educational work has been widely praised, and it received national recognition in 1966 when the Israel Prize for Education [the country's highest award in this field] was awarded to the Israel Defense Forces. The Nahal, which combines military training and agricultural settlement, also provides teachers for border villages who contribute to their social and cultural development. These are only some examples of the Israel Defense Forces' uniqueness. . . .

What are some other examples?

Almost all of Israel's youth are called to the colors, be they educated or not, skilled or not, native-born or not, fluent in Hebrew or not. Where necessary, Zahal begins or expands the process of making educated people out of uneducated ones and skilled people out of unskilled ones.

All conscripts who need it get training in the national language, history, and geography, as well as in the three R's. Those without primary school diplomas, usually stemming from the Oriental communities, are posted to the Military School for Formal Education, popularly known as the Marcus School, which is in a beautiful setting near the Dan Carmel Hotel in Haifa overlooking the Mediterranean. There they take a three-months course taught by female soldiers. The classes are small —usually two teachers for twelve students, as compared to a ratio of one teacher to about thirty-five students in the regular civilian school system. Also, unlike the latter school system, with its heavy emphasis on rote learning, memorization, and traditional methods, the Marcus School stresses thinking for oneself, the how and why of learning, and is filled with such modern teaching aids as movies, slide shows, and teaching machines. And most important of all, the students are under military jurisdiction and discipline. They live where they learn, and their learning day is from ten to twelve hours, six days a week.

At first, the course was given to a soldier immediately upon his induction. The results were disastrous. One reason is that for some, Camp Marcus reopens the painful wounds of earlier school failures. A second is that the recruits—raw, undisciplined, and mostly from Islamic countries—resented having a woman in authority over them. Now the course is given at the end of a soldier's service, when he is older, more mature, more motivated, more socially integrated, and more disciplined. When I visited the school, I found that ninety percent of its students came from disadvantaged families from such countries as Morocco, Iraq, Tunisia, Yemen, Turkey, Iran, Libya, Algeria, and Egypt. Some of them were new immigrants, others juvenile delinquents. Yet they make the grade. They have to, for they don't get their discharge until they do.

But obviously, it's only a start. Three short months can't possibly give semi-literate soldiers all they need to get on in life. But they can help them defeat hopelessness and encourage them to continue some kind of formal education after their release. Certainly the more mature and motivated soldiers do so. As one of them said:

> Sure, every one who's seen a movie wants to get on in life, but there [at a development town where he eked out a living on relief work] I didn't know how to go about it. Once I joined the carpentry course, but it was no good. . . . Not without Hebrew and doing sums quickly . . . I gave up. . . . Well, now I won't give up. I may not be a scholar when I leave but I can already read an easy newspaper and understand a textbook that isn't too difficult.

Another Army vehicle for educational socialization and integration is Gadna, a contraction of the Hebrew words Ge'dudei

Noar (Youth Battalions). It operates in high schools, teachers' seminaries, technical schools, maritime schools, agricultural schools, etc. It plays an active role in Israeli youth movements, youth centers, and institutions and courses organized by the Council of Working Women, the Ministry of Labor, and the Ministry of Social Welfare. Its eight aims, as listed in an official brochure published by the Ministry of Defense Publishing House, are: "Getting to Know and Love the Homeland," "Loyalty to the Nation and the State," "Consciousness of Security," "Physical Fitness and Target Shooting," "Resourcefulness in the Field," "Order and Discipline," "Commanding and Instruction Qualities," and "Esprit de Corps and Comradeship." All of these aims are channeled into the main purpose of training young teen-agers for pioneering and for specialized military and technical skills. For example, Air-Gadna members learn how to fly gliders and light aircraft. In addition to its own training bases, Gadna has its own farm, which prepares people for Nahal, the Army's agricultural arm; an acclaimed youth symphony orchestra, weekly radio programs, and its own wall newspaper and bi-weekly magazine.

Though Gadna is jointly run by the Ministry of Education and the Ministry of Defense, the latter can veto any changes proposed by the former that the military does not like. Thus when officials in the Education Ministry complained in early 1971 that the ten to fifteen percent of the school schedule devoted to Gadna activities was too much, Moshe Netzer, the head of the Youth and Nahal Division of the Ministry of Defense, said that "any decision which the Ministry of Education reaches is subject to military approval." And in reporting the matter, the *Jerusalem Post* said: "The army . . . is expected to have the last word."

Besides involvement in primary and secondary school education, Zahal has some programs at the university level. "Scores" of regular officers are sent each year to Israeli and foreign universities to take degrees. A very limited number of young men who want to study such militarily useful subjects as medicine, dentistry, and aeronautics, are allowed to join what is called the Academic Reserve. Academic reservists must first enlist in the Army at eighteen and pass an intensive basic-training course. Only then can they start their university studies as "soldiers on special leave." Upon graduation, they return to the Army and use their professional training as the Army directs.

Zahal also helps high school dropouts or those who failed to pass the national matriculation exam required of all students who aspire to a college education. Matriculation classes are available at military bases and in the larger centers of population; "secondary education by correspondence," in the words of an Army document, "is more ubiquitous and ampler from year to year." The Army sends forty-five students a year to the Hebrew University's Pre-Academic Center to remove scholastic deficiencies that prevent them from being admitted to college. It also gives some financial help to a number of discharged soldiers who go to the Center each year. Thus the Army tries to do its share in giving young Israelis a second chance by salvaging as many of them as possible for a college career. Additionally, the Haifa Technion, "as an expression of gratitude to the Army for its brilliant achievements during the Six Day War," has since 1968 awarded scholarships to soldiers recommended by the Army.

Standing between primary and university education is vocational training—so important to both deevloped and developing societies. Here the Israeli Army plays a central role. Since a modern army needs so many skills that are also required in civilian life—electricians, mechanics, drivers, office workers, and so on—Zahal has a vast vocational education program, perhaps the largest in the country. The Air Force's Technical College in Haifa trains aircraft ground crews "by the thousands." Ten percent of the graduates of the Navy's nautical school can opt for positions in the merchant marine in place of service in the Navy. And from time to time one sees wall posters and advertisements such as this one which appeared in the newspaper *Ma'ariv* accompanied by the picture of two soldiers working over a drafting board;

129

Israel Defense Forces—Study at the Technical Boarding School of the Ordnance Corps—Information Meetings—Parents and young men interested in details about opportunities for studying at the Technical Boarding School of the Ordnance Corps are invited to a meeting with the School's Commandant at the Jerusalem Mobilization Office on May 10, . . . at the Tel-Aviv Mobilization Office on May 12, . . . at the Haifa Mobilization Office on May 17. . . . Details and registration at all regional Mobilization Offices. Written particulars may be obtained by contacting Military Post Office Sh/2375, Israel Defense Forces.

The Ordinance Corps' Technical Boarding School (or pnimia, as a boarding school is called in Hebrew) brings to mind Israel's two pnimiot zvaiot, one near Tel-Aviv and the other near Haifa. In English these two institutions are called military academies. But they are really military high schools, where a small number of Israel's future Army officers go. In fact, they are not even military high schools as much as they are military-civilian high schools, and this is the important point. For reasons both of "demilitarizing" the military and of keeping the professional army as much a part and servant of civilian society as possible, Israel has very deliberately chosen *not* to have a college-level military academy in the usual sense.

As a former Commandant of the school near Tel-Aviv once put it, "If the Army had decided to do so, it would have been very simple to get together some teachers and open our own separate school. But this is precisely what was not wanted." Instead, the cadets in the Tel-Aviv area attend classes in the mornings and early afternoons at the famous Herzliah High School in Tel-Aviv and those in the Haifa area do the same thing at the equally prestigious Reali High School in Haifa. They follow the regular curriculum and standards that the civilian boys and girls at these schools must follow. While they are at the Herzliah and Reali schools, the cadets wear civilian clothes. It is only after they get back to the pnimia, at about two in the afternoon, that they change into military uniforms and begin their Army studies as well as do their civilian home-

work. After four years at the pnimia—for which their parents
pay—the boys graduate as corporals and go on to Officers
Training School.

Graduating with the exalted rank of corporal tells us a
great deal about the Israeli approach to officership and the
expected relationship between officers and the men they must
lead. The motto of the officer corps is *Acharei* (After Me!).
And Israelis—even military boarding school graduates—generally can become officers only by climbing the ranks from enlisted
man to non-commissioned officer to regular or reserve officer. In
short, the whole purpose is to integrate the citizen into the
soldiery and the Army into the citizenry. That is why future
officers from the pnimia sit in the same classes with future professionals and future housewives.

As far as integration within the Army is concerned, except
for the (non-Jewish) Minorities Unit, the policy is to mix
members from different ethnic groups, social classes, and
economic backgrounds in each military component of any size.
For many Israelis, the Army is the first, last, and only place
where such mixing, especially of Ashkenazim and Sephardim,
occurs on a daily, more or less permanent, basis. As for the
Army and immigrant absorption, from time to time officers taking courses on The Jewish People Today meet new immigrants
arriving at Haifa port or Lod airport. They follow the newcomers' path of integration from ship or plane to port or airport
processing center to temporary absorption center to permanent
place of residence and work. Sometimes Army units "adopt"
groups of new immigrants, such as the adoption of immigrants
living in the absorption center in Pardess Hanna by soldiers
of a Nahal unit in northern Israel. The get-togethers between
"old" soldiers and new immigrants do a great deal to dispel
misconceptions between the two, especially over housing and
other aid given to newcomers but not to oldtimers.

The *Israel Digest* of January 5, 1973 quotes the reactions of
a male sergeant and a lady soldier in the Nahal unit to these
encounters with the immigrants. Said the sergeant: "What
one hears about the privileges granted to newcomers has turned

out to be largely exaggerated. Now I know that they have as many problems, if not more, than we do. It's not an easy thing to settle down in a new country and to learn a new language." Said the lady soldier: "We need the immigrants as much as they need Israel. Now I know that they're not taking away a house from me, or getting a car at my father's expense. We are doing our best to make them feel wanted and at home."

A society that is immigrant-laden, highly urbanized, very heterogeneous, rapidly changing, and racing toward industrialization to boot, often spawns juvenile delinquency. Modern Israel is no exception. We discussed earlier the traumatic effect which rejection for military service has on many Israeli young people. We also mentioned the Israeli "Black Panthers" and the fact that one of their principal complaints is that a record of juvenile delinquency has usually been enough to keep them out of the Army and from social acceptance and the better civilian jobs that they want and need. Defense Minister Dayan, when he was Chief of Staff in the 1950's, opposed non-military activities by the Army, and Education Minister Allon, himself a former general in the 1940's, once responded to a question about the Army's helping juvenile delinquents by saying: "I don't think we ought to ask the Army to take on something like this." But by the end of 1970 and the beginning of 1971 public pressure to do something about the problem became too great for the Army to ignore. On March 2, 1971 the *Jerusalem Post* editoralized:

> The army is not an institution for social service, but there is genuine pathos in the tale of the boy who is rejected by the army "until he has worked for a year" because he is marked down as a juvenile delinquent, and who protests that good jobs and training courses are not open to anyone who was rejected by the army on such grounds, that such rejection becomes an insuperable stigma.

> It is good to know that the Labor Ministry is now offering psychotechnical tests to young people looking for jobs . . . We surely have no right to let a boy of eighteen feel that an

offense committed at fifteen has effectively barred him from normal society. If he comes to believe, as a result, that Matzpen [the anti-Israel Israeli new left organization] is his only friend in the world we shall have only ourselves to blame. . . .

Similarly, on March 12 the *Post* carried this letter from one of its readers: "I have just read the article 'Street Gangs' . . . and was surprised to find that young men (or women) who 'tangle with the police and have a record' are rejected by the Army. This is a most short-sighted policy. I'm sure the great majority of these unfortunate boys and girls would be rehabilitated if given a chance to serve their country."

By the Spring of 1971 Zahal, at the urging of the Minister of Labor and the Minister of Social Welfare, agreed not only to provide counselling, training, employment, food, overalls, a small salary, and transport to Army workshops for some 1500 "problem youngsters," but it also recruited some men with criminal records. Twenty inmates from the Tel Mond juvenile jail were actually inducted into the Armored Corps on an experimental basis at the end of 1971. At the end of 1972 the Police Minister Shlomo Hillel announced that some 10,000 Israeli youngsters are arrested each year for various crimes but that only about 250 of them are sentenced to jail. He also announced that about half of the 150 juvenile offenders who were released from prison during the preceding eighteen months to join the Army had adjusted. The other half didn't "make it" in the Army. Some of these even went back to crime. In the Summer of 1973 some forty Gadna youth leaders were trained to go into distressed areas to challenge the street gangs and work with the so-called "marginal youth." But it is too early to know and evaluate the results of this Army- and Education Ministry-sponsored effort.

Six months before the Six Day War the University of Chicago held a conference on the draft. The papers presented were later published in a book, *The Draft: A Handbook of Facts and Alternatives,* edited by Chicago Professor Sol Tax. One of the papers is called "Education Processes in the Israel Defense Forces" and it was written by Colonel Mordechai M. Bar-On, I.D.F.'s Chief Education Officer at the time. Colonel Bar-On concluded his address with passages from a letter from a young officer to his girl on the day of his discharge from Zahal. In somewhat idealized terms, the letter expresses what Zahal seeks to accomplish in absorbing, integrating, and maturing the young people of Israel:

> Well, this day is over too, this day to which I had looked forward so much wherever I was throughout the last three years. And now a new day has come . . . I do not know whether I will have another day like this, that concludes a whole period with all that happened within it, with hard and tiring work, powerful experiences, moments of pain and worry, moments of expectation and fear, the friendship of many, occasional hatred, a thousand and one human experiences.

> How often I have wanted to write and tell you about all that the army has given me, about how great the distance is between Uri of those times and Uri of now. I went into the army as a young boy, naïve, believing in many values with great snowwhite expectations: the kind of man who grows up on the margin of life and who has hardly ever known what disappointment means. And who is Uri of today? Almost a totally different person. I come out of the army as an adult who has already gone through the first stages in his road through life, and with ideas which may perhaps even be regarded as new.

> My hopes have remained the same, but much of what surrounds them has changed. The experience which I have acquired, the experience within the new society is enormous. It was a giant test of my strength, my balance, my ability to work with people, my ability to stand up without anybody pushing me from behind.

> What kind of a person I am nowadays is hard to define, but I am much more than the boy of those days. Today I know that our world is a combination of colors and tints which no one can separate, that there is nothing in which there is not something positive and something negative all mixed together, that everywhere there are lights and shades, and that

sometimes even people who differ from you in their views and in the background of their lives, may be right, each in his own way.

Out of myself and out of my osbservation and contact with others, I have learnt a little of what kind of creature man is. Sometimes he is petty and miserable, gives in to small things, and sometimes he achieves unimagined heights.

From the army, which is the forge of discipline to the very end for him who carries out the order as well as he who gives it, I have come with more understanding of what is really the true meaning of freedom and democracy.

11

The Army
and Politics

IN THE DAYS of British-ruled Palestine, the Jewish underground was highly politicized. There was the Haganah, the fighting force of the Yishuv, or Jewish Community, under the control of Mapai, the Socialist-Zionist party that has dominated Israeli politics to this very day. There was the Palmach, the left-of-Mapai force of the Achdut Avodah (Labor Unity) party, which wanted a people's army politically and philosophically oriented to the kibbutz. There were the Irgun and the Stern Gang, whose members had a political approach resppectively much farther to the right than either the Haganah or the Palmach.

With the creation of Israel, David Ben-Gurion, who was her first Prime Minister and Defense Minister for quite a long while, decreed the end of military-separatist groupings. He did away with the Palmach as a distinct unit and literally forced the dissolution of the dissident Irgun and Stern Gang organizations, allowing their members to be incorporated into Zahal, the new army of the new state.

In a statement to his party, during one of its interminable internal debates, he said: "All my life I have been a member of the party and of the Histadrut [the labor union federation] and—so I believe—I shall remain one for the rest of my life. I am ready to fight for the interests of the party and Histadrut. But there is one body in the Yishuv in which I shall never be reconciled to any barrier or party or organizational distinction between one Jew and another, and that is the Army. Within the Army I am not prepared to recognize either Histadrut or party." On its face the statement's meaning is clear: Zahal would be based on merit alone, and pure professionalism would replace party politics.

Many years later, in February 1969, Defense Minister Moshe Dayan read out to the Parliament some of the salient passages of Army Regulation No. 33.0116, concerning political participation by Israeli soldiers:

A soldier may be a member of any association or party which exists legally in the State, but must avoid all activity in these bodies apart from the following:

A soldier may be present at a meeting or a convention of the association or party as above, but:

A soldier may not actively participate as a speaker, member of the presidium, or fulfill any other active function in the meeting or convention and in the preparations for them.

A soldier may not take part in a military gathering or soldiers' meetings which are held by a body which is not military, or an unauthorized military body. He is also not allowed to discuss military subjects at any meeting or convention without the permission of his superiors.

A soldier will not discuss in public, orally or in writing, in circumstances which give the said discussion a public character, any political question (or question which may be interpreted as political) except as stated below.

A soldier may not accept any invitation from an association, party or any other public or civil body, to take an active part in any meeting, party or any other ceremonial occasion, as a representative of the army. He will also not accept any such invitation under circumstances in which his participation or presence may be interpreted as representing the army, even if the invitation is meant for him in a direct and personal manner, except if the representative function was given to him by virtue of his appointment or a special authorization from the Chief of Staff or the head of the Manpower Division of the General Staff, or, in the case of soldiers who are present in the course of their duty in countries to which Israel Defense Forces attachés are accredited, by an I.D.F. attaché, in accordance with the nature of the activity.

One wonders, of course, how these efforts at depoliticizing the Israeli Army have met the tests of time and of reality both in the period between Ben-Gurion and Dayan, as well as the period between Dayan and now. But before we can get some answers we need to make some definitions and distinctions.

Politics is the relationship of people to governmental power. Since a nation's army is a subunit of its governing system, even a "non-political" army is involved in politics: the politics of economics, the politics of administration, the politics of weaponry, the politics of manpower, the politics of strategy, and, above all, *the politics of advice!* For an army that gives no military advice to the nation's political leaders is not doing its job properly. An army that gives such advice is involved in politics, whether it likes it or not. So that the problem of civil-military relations exists in all states, dictatorial as well as democratic, and the question thus becomes: Does the military tail wag the civilian dog or is it the other way around? And if it is the other way around, how do the civil authorities manage it, especially in a country like Israel where it is already agreed that "between us and death stands only Zahal, Zahal alone?"

As for distinctions, when a political scientist talks about civil-military relations and the political role of the army, he is talking about the officer corps. In Israel's case, that means the Chief of Staff, the members of the General Staff, and certain other generals and colonels. Second, a distinction has to be made between (1) the relationship between the Army's high command and the Cabinet and the Knesset, (2) political acts or aspirations of officers on active duty, especially any contact between them and the political parties, (3) the political influence of retired senior officers, and (4) the long-term impact of the Army on Israeli democracy—in other words, the question of militarism. Let us begin with the Chief of Staff.

In the United States it is doubtful that the President, in appointing the uniformed heads of each of the services or the Chairman of the Joint Chiefs of Staff, cares very much whether any of these generals or admirals is a registered Republican or Democrat. It is certainly not a tradition that Democratic Presidents choose only Democratic generals and Republican Presidents only Republican generals. But in Israel the historical fact is that none of her nine Chiefs of Staff to date—Ya'acov Dori, Yigal Yadin, Mordechai Makleff, Moshe Dayan, Haim Laskov, Zvi Zur, Yitzchak Rabin, Haim Bar-Lev, and David Elazar— could have been named to the post if he was perceived as someone at odds with the general socialist-kibbutz-Histadrut orientation of the major political party that has ruled Israel since her inception. That being the case—and especially since the Labor Party won again in the recent parliamentary elections—no Israeli general who aspires to become a future Chief of Staff can afford to be regarded as anti-labor, anti-socialist, or anti-kibbutz if he is serious about achieving his aspiration. This is true no matter how popular he is with the public or how brilliant he is as a military strategist or tactician.

Once appointed, how does a Chief of Staff, and the members of the General Staff, relate to the Israeli Cabinet and Knesset? The Chief of Staff, as well as the Chief of Military Intelligence, meets with the Knesset's Defense and Foreign Affairs Committee at least once a month. They also report regularly to the Finance Committee. When called upon, they attend Cabinet meetings where, Major General Eliahu Ze'ira, the current intelligence chief, told me in an interview on

December 24, 1972, they "have a great deal of influence on government policy." (One of the reasons for this influence may be Israel's lack of multiple intelligence agencies. The only official intelligence agency is Miltary Intelligence. This means that Military Intelligence people in Israel have a burden and responsibility that their counterparts in the armies of other democratic states do not have: they are the only ones who make intelligence assessments for the government. As General Ze'ira freely admitted: "If we are right, we are very right. But if we are wrong, we are very wrong. For there is no way of comparing our assessments of issues and personalities with civilian agencies.")

At first glance, it would appear that the Knesset has a great deal of control over Zahal. There are the regular meetings between top Army leaders and the Knesset's Defense and Foreign Affairs Committee. That Committee is composed of the top leaders of the country's major political parties, all of whom take their Committee assignment very seriously. In a recent Knesset, there were nineteen members on the Committee. Ten of them were ex-Cabinet ministers and one a former Supreme Court justice. As someone very close to the Committee put it to me privately: "If the Committee never says 'no' to Zahal, it is not because it is subservient. It is because, before making their decision, the members reach a consensus with the Cabinet. Israel has a parliamentary-cabinet system of government where the legislative parties control their ministers in the Cabinet. Since the members of the Knesset's Defense and Foreign Affairs Committee are the 'Number 1's' in their respective parties, consensus between the executive and legislative branches is easily obtainable and civilian control of the military is maintained."

But just how accurate is this first glance? True, under a Cabinet system each government minister, including the Defense Minister, attends meetings of the legislature and is subject to the questions and queries of its members. But in a Cabinet system the executive usually dominates the legislature, especially if it has a big enough majority in Parliament. And in the Israeli system the Defense Minister (for the time being, at least, the tradition that the Prime Minister is also the Defense Minister has been broken) usually dominates the Cabinet on military matters.

Under Israeli Law, a law that was passed when the Prime Minister and the Defense Minister were the same person, defense policy lies wholly within the province of the Defense Minister. He executes the Knesset's laws concerning the Army. He issues, or directs the issuance, of pertinent Army regulations. He implements the grand decisions taken by the Cabinet as a whole. But as Columbia University Professor J. C. Hurewitz has observed in his book *Middle East Politics: The Military Dimension*:

> [The Defense Minister] . . . serves, in effect, as the commander-in-chief of the armed forces, although his office does not expressly carry the title. Under the law, the defense minister need not consult his cabinet colleagues or procure Knesset endorsement before making major decisions, even the decision to mobilize the reserve brigades. He must, it is true, immediately bring such a mobilization order to the attention of the Knesset Committee on . . . [Defense and Foreign Affairs], which may confirm the order, or modify it, or withhold confirmation, or refer it to the plenary Knesset. However, in the event of a situation that seems to demand mobilization, is the Knesset likely to reverse the order of the defense minister?

If Israeli law and tradition give to the Defense Minister the heavy responsibility of keeping the military out of politics, that responsibility becomes heaviest when the post is held by someone like Moshe Dayan, the present incumbent. He is not the first Israeli Defense Minister who is not simultaneously the Prime Minister. Pinchas Levon holds that distinction. But whereas Prime Minister David Ben-Gurion freely appointed Lavon, Prime Minister Levi Eshkol, Golda Meir's predecessor, picked Dayan not because he really wanted to—fierce public pressure on the eve of the Six Day War forced him to. One of those who led the pressure was the Old Man himself, who since his retirement from politics had turned against his former colleague. "The nation," said Ben-Gurion, "should have some-one in the government [particularly in the Defense portfolio] in whom they have faith, and therefore Moshe should join it. . . . Moshe's entry into the Cabinet will also inject new trust and confidence in the Army. . . . "

Curiously, a reversal of the attitudes of Eshkol and Dayan occurred when the latter took office. According to Dayan's biographer, Shabtai Teveth, his first reactions upon becoming the Defense Minister and stewarding the Six Day War was that Zahal should *not* go all the way to the Suez Canal, should *not* capture the Old City of Jerusalem, and should *not* open up a Syrian front. But, Teveth wrote in his book, *Moshe Dayan*:

> Eshkol who as Minister of Defense had been unsure and hesitant became aggressive and decisive from the moment Dayan assumed his post and Zahal reaped its first victories. On the very first day of the war, June 5, he demanded that "the sources of the Jordan be seized," in other words, that war be launched against Syria. On the other hand, Dayan who as Chief of Staff was known for his eagerness for battle and had been appointed Minister of Defense because the nation had faith in his leadership in time of war now became so moderate and wary as to arouse bitter resentment in the government, the army, and large sections of the population.

But let us return to the differences not between Dayan and Eshkol but between Dayan and Lavon. These had much greater implications for civil-military relations in Israel. Lavon was a civilian, a brilliant Labor Party thinker. He had no prior experience in military matters and no old and loyal friends in the Army or the Defense Ministry. Dayan, on the other hand, had spent half a lifetime in the Army, where he rose to be its most independent-acting and politically oriented Chief of Staff. Once, in the middle of very delicate Foreign Ministry negotiations with Canada, he ordered on his own initiative an enormous retaliatory raid across the border. As a result, Canada broke off the talks and Israel did not get the planes she was trying to buy. Further, Dayan had great support within the Army. Lavon never did. In fact, certain Zahal elements helped to engineer his political downfall. In the so-called Lavon Affair, which occurred when Dayan was Chief of Staff, Lavon was unjustly accused of being responsible for a "security mishap" involving an unsuccessful sabotage attempt on the offices of the United States Information Agency in Cairo. Lavon neither planned nor knew about the operation. Those in the military, especially in the intelligence service, who helped to smear Lavon—he was later absolved of all responsibility for the mishap but was ruined politically anyway—did so because they did not like his attempts to change the old way of doing things.

Lavon tried to be the Robert S. McNamara of Israel. Like McNamara, he tried to get on top, and stay on top, of both the Ministry of Defense and the uniformed service. He wanted to be the supreme authority on defense matters, as Ben-Gurion had been before him. But he had none of Ben-Gurion's charisma, style, respect, or popularity within the Army. And he broke B.G.'s precedent of not interfering with the uniformed specialists' decisions on which weapons to buy. Like McNamara, Lavon wanted the Defense Minister to *really* oversee and control Zahal. Whereas McNamara succeeded in somewhat controlling the American military apparatus, Lavon failed completely in Israel, especially in his attempt to dominate Zahal. The Israeli Army is not yet ready for a Hebrew-speaking McNamara, nor, for that matter, are the Cabinet, the Knesset, and the people of Israel. So, even under Dayan, the Chief of Staff and his senior colleagues still have the last word on military strategy and tactics. However, the Defense Ministry, as an administrative unit in the government bureaucracy, has built its own empire in logistics, supply, and the development of military industry.

As might be expected, the military in Israel doesn't always see the problem of civil-military relations in the same light as those who have not spent a good deal of their lives in uniform. In early 1973 Chief of Staff David Elazar answered the criticism that Zahal was too detached from civilian control by saying that the present arrangement is the "classic example of what the relations between the military and the government should be in any advanced democratic country."

But former Quartermaster-General Mattatyahu Peled, now an Arabic and Arab affairs specialist at Tel-Aviv University, did not like the equilibrium established between the political and military leaders of Israel when he wrote an important article about the Six Day War for the May 16, 1969 issue of the Hebrew daily *Ma'ariv*. On the "question of the relations between the General Staff and the government," Peled says:

> For many years I had felt that the General Staff was not fulfilling properly its constitutional role within the framework of Israel democracy, in that it was not helping the government crystalize defense policy. Over the years, an extremely strict interpretation of the concept of keeping the military out of politics had taken hold. In my opinion, this was a very serious mistake. If the top echelons of the Finance Ministry helped the government to crystallize fiscal policy and the Foreign Ministry's top echelons helped the government to crystallize foreign policy—who was to fulfill this role in the area of national security? After all, Zahal's top echelons consisted of people who over many years had studied military and security matters at government expense, so that the government should benefit from the experience and know-how they had acquired.
>
> I don't mean to say that the military leadership should be permitted to dictate security policy to the government— only that it must be called in by the government to present data, assessments, concepts, and ideas on which the government can base its conclusions.
>
> In actual fact, the contact between the Zahal leadership and the government was restricted to the regular contacts between the Chief of Staff and the Defense Minister, and the occasional participation of the Chief of Staff in Cabinet meetings—mainly in order to listen and to report. . . .

. . . Mr. Eshkol was not satisfied with this arrangement. He did not feel comfortable about always having to confront the Chief of Staff with practically nothing to say in view of the tremendous weight which the Chief of Staff carried in the matters they were discussing, at a time when he (Eshkol) was perhaps considering the broader ramifications of security considerations. . . . Mr. Eshkol felt he had no "forum" with which to discuss and consider the problems at hand in order to arrive at a decision. I remember that once, at a personal meeting, he asked me what I thought about this. I agreed with him and I pointed out that the problem had been solved in different ways in different countries, but that all the solutions had in common the principle of a "national defense council," or a "supreme command council," which meets from time to time to consider the broader ramifications of security. . . .

The real problem underlying General Peled's discussion is not the administrative format—Chief of Staff, a National Security Council, or what have you—through which the Army makes its views known to the government. It is the distinction between military persuasion and military pressure. "Pressure" and "persuasion" are relative and subjective terms. What may appear to one civilian leader (or critic) as an energetic presentation of the military's views, may look to another like undisguised and unmitigated coercion. Time and circumstances also affect the persuasion-pressure differential. During the fearful weeks before the Six Day War—Israel won the war so most foreigners don't know or remember that fear and doubt gripped the country in April and May of 1967—the military did everything it could to influence the government to attack the Egyptian forces concentrated in the Sinai. General Peled admits it openly. It was "necessary to persuade the Cabinet Ministers that if only they had the courage to decide, Zahal would do its job to the full. I did everything I could in this respect."

And that is exactly the point. Zahal can try to persuade but it cannot and does not dictate. While its words may be very carefully listened to, it does not have the final word. If the government asks the Army General Staff about the present borders, the latter would probably say that they are ideal and should be kept. But if the government decides not to keep them, there is no doubt that the Army will go along with that decision. For, as demonstrated by the 1973 Yom Kippur War and the ensuing cease-fire talks at Kilometer 101 in Egypt and the peace negotiations in Geneva, Israeli decisions about when and where to go to war, when to wait, whom to strike, when and how and with whom to make peace are political decisions. They are made by the civilian Cabinet, which takes full responsibility for them. In fact, Tourism Minister Moshe Kol once complained that the Cabinet spent so much time on matters related to military affairs and foreign policy that little time was left at its meetings for pressing domestic issues.

As for our second concern—political activity by officers on active duty—there has been none to speak of, except for episodes in 1969 and 1973. The first episode was an effort by one of the political parties to introduce and maintain an "information circle" within Zahal. It came to light in January 1969, when the Israeli Cabinet, as a gesture of national unity that had begun just before the Six Day War, was still composed of all of the country's major parties from the non-Communist left to the center and the right. It created commotion in the military, the Cabinet, the Parliament, the press, and the parties, including the offending Labor Party.

The facts are briefly these. "Without bothering," in the words of Moshe Dayan, "to pick up a telephone and ask the Defense Minister what he thought about this circle," Yisrael Granitt, an ex-Army colonel and assistant to Pinchas Sapir, who was then the Secretary-General of the Labor Party, organized an information circle for senior Army officers. The Independent Liberals demanded stricter standing orders to keep politics out of the Army and asked for a Knesset debate. Four Gahal members of the Knesset's Defense and Foreign Affairs Committee wired Prime Minister Eshkol, Defense Minister Dayan, and other members of the Cabinet insisting on "immediate steps to block the introduction of politics into the army." At a meeting in Tel-Aviv, Elimelech Rimalt, chairman of the Liberals, said: "If we do not manage by parliamentary and public measures to prevent this Labor Party initiative then I personally think that Gahal should review its continued membership in the Cabinet." A *Jerusalem Post* columnist wrote that if such circles were made legal, it "would mean . . . that not only the Labor Party would hold its meetings, but that every other party would be equally entitled to arrange meetings to indoctrinate soldiers. When the party meetings were over the arguments would be carried back into barracks and mess rooms and the good-humored comradeship in the army, on which lives often depend, might be gravely threatened in an election year." And the *Post* editorialized:

> Israel has been able to take pride in the fact that its army, like its judiciary, has been placed above and beyond politics. . . .

> . . . [The] sense of removal from politics has become a fundamental part of the army's ideological fabric. It is part of the self-image of every officer and every enlisted man. It is also an essential component of the esteem in which the army is held by the nation. For here the political and ideological differences which divide the body politic are transcended. Here the basic unity of the nation is affirmed. . . .

> When the lines between the politicians and the military become blurred the rot sets in. Partisan political values become more important than military values. The nature of an officer's political loyalties become more important than the level of his professional competence. The links of respect between officers and their men dissolve.

> The inevitable result is that the military takes over politics, sweeping away democracy, and politics takes over the military, sweeping away security.

> The ill-considered effort of a senior officer in the Reserves

therefore deserves all the condemnation it has been accorded both in and outside the Labor Party. . . .

Presumably the army and the Defense Ministry will seek to tighten the regulations which lay down the prohibitions of political activity. But it is not with formalities that integrity and security lie.

What is needed is for the Cabinet, the Knesset and the . . . Labor Party to reject and censure this dangerous attempt to undermine a cardinal tenet of the nation's political principles, and a fundamental ingredient of its security.

That editorial appeared on January 24, 1969. Yet when the Labor Party's Leadership Bureau met three weeks later, the issue was far from settled. Pinchas Sapir noted that similar circles had been around for twenty years under the party's Department for Mobilized Men. Shimon Peres deplored the failure to consult with Defense Minister Dayan and with other high-ranking party officials. In any case, he thought the party's activity within the Army should cease. Golda Meir (who was not Prime Minister at the time) said she used to, when she was Foreign Minister, talk to rallies of officers and saw no objection. When someone at the meeting pointed out that David Ben-Gurion had always been against such rallies, she answered: "If I had known that Ben-Gurion opposed them, I never would have attended such rallies." Gad Ya'acobi strongly opposed the Army information or political circle and pressed for a decision by the Leadership Bureau against it. On the other hand, Education Minister, Zalman Aranne, called the hubbub of the opposition parties "pure hypocrisy."

By the Spring of 1969, the issue vanished from public view. The regulations and prohibitions against party activity in the Army, which the *Post* and others called for, were apparently implemented. For Israel is a very small country, where the only secrets kept for long are military secrets. She has a plethora of political parties and factions and a free and ferreting press. If any group had tried to repeat the "information circle caper," it would have been uncovered and undone long before now.

The second episode—or more correctly, series of episodes—resulted from the Yom Kippur War. That war was unique in that: (1) it delayed Israel's national elections until December 31, 1973, (2) it caught the Israeli's off-guard, and (3) it necessitated the call-up of some retired generals who were already in, or were about to enter, politics—men like Haim Bar-Lev, the Minister of Commerce and Industry in the Labor-dominated government and Ariel Sharon, the general who trapped the Egyptian Third Army on the other side of the Suez Canal and who was one of the architects of the Likud opposition grouping that did so well in the elections.

The war was also unique in that it sparked, in the words of one Israeli observer, "the sudden unprecedented spate of criticism and accusations by senior military officers against each other or the General Staff and the airing of these grievances, including uncensored interviews in the press while the fighting was still in progress . . . " The principal offenders were the two reserve generals mentioned above, particularly "Arik" Sharon. If left unchecked and if repeated, such behavior could pose a danger to democracy in Israel, or at least push military influence quite close to the end of acceptable limits.

Professor Abel Jacob of the City University of New York addressed himself to the danger in a letter to the *New York Times,* published on December 18, 1973. In it he wrote:

> The recent conflict in the Middle East highlighted a particularly important problem for Israeli society: the increasing participation of military men turned politicians who are recalled to military duty during times of crisis.

> The outstanding example is Maj. Gen. Ariel (Arik) Sharon, who left the army in July and was recalled to military duty for the Yom Kippur war. His strong criticism of Israel's senior military officers, especially the ones directly above him, . . . is a new development in Israel's history.

There is little doubt that Arik Sharon was motivated by political considerations since after leaving the army he had formed the Likud . . . to prepare for the forthcoming elections. His criticism was directed not only at military matters but also at political and diplomatic ones. He stated that the government was too concerned with the Soviet threat and too anxious to please the Americans.

The problem here is a new version on the theme of the role of the military in politics.

In most cases we view the problem thus: Military men usurp political power and remain in power indefinitely. In this case, the former military officer entered politics in an accepted, legitimate fashion and then, due to circumstances, was put back into uniform. However, his politicization had already taken hold when he found himself in uniform again.

Professor Jacob's solution to this problem is a law that would keep retired officers out of the political arena "for a sufficient period of time, say five years or so, in order to weaken their contacts with the professional military."

The third question regarding civil-military relations is why retired Zahal officers are attracted to the rough-and-tumble, hurly-burly world of Israeli party politics and why the political parties try so hard to attract them to that world.

As already indicated in the chapter on the post-retirement careers of ex-Zahalniks, the number and percentage who have entered active politics is small. However, since the Six Day War it has been growing. And those who have "parachuted into politics," as Israeli political slang phrases it, have often— not always—landed in the Knesset or even the Cabinet on their very first jump. When this happens, civilian party workers who have given a lifetime to the party don't like it and are increasingly saying so. If they can't prevent a "parachute jump," they try to neutralize or isolate the officer after he's made his jump.

Retired officers with political ambitions are aware of this reaction but many of them simply don't care. "Of course the

Haim Bar-Lev, who served as Chief of Staff just before the present one, David Elazar. For Bar-Lev's entry into the Cabinet as Minister of Commerce and Industry in 1972 goes to the very heart of the question of what is the proper method—not only legally but ethically as well—of a high general parachuting into high politics.

Bar-Lev is not the first Chief of Staff to enter an Israeli Cabinet. Moshe Dayan is. But whereas Dayan served a period of political apprenticeship between leaving the Army and joining the government, Bar-Lev went almost directly from his military to his government post. Actually, the general—he was never Chief of Staff—who joined a Cabinet within twenty-four hours of his Army retirement is Ezer Weizman. That was in 1969, when there was a government of national unity. It was because of him that the "100-days rule" between leaving the civil service and running for the Parliament was extended to retired Army officers seeking seats in the Knesset. In Israel, however, one doesn't need to be elected to the Knesset in order to be a Cabinet minister. The rule does not therefore apply to such Cabinet members. Nevertheless, Premier Golda Meir waited several months before inviting Bar-Lev to join her government.

Pros and cons about generals in the government have been expressed by individual civilians and military men. Editorialists in the Israeli newspapers *Omer* and the *Jerusalem Post* warmly welcomed Bar-Lev's taking over the Ministry of Commerce and Industry. The *Post's* noted columnist Lea Ben Dor wrote on July 24, 1973: "We have no right to close the doors to senior public positions to these [Army] men who have been in the public service all their lives. It would also be an irresponsible waste of manpower." The Histadrut's Ben-Aharon attacked "troublemakers, slanderers, wicked tongues who allege I oppose the entry of former army commanders into political life. I have never done so," he said. Moshe Dayan said, when there were reports in 1971 of both Bar-Lev and Yitzchak Rabin (the Chief of Staff during the 1967 war) joining the Cabinet: "I think both will make excellent ministers. There are no principles involved here . . . Some chiefs of staff [himself] have become ministers, others haven't. I may only have reservations about chiefs of staff . . . having their military glory exploited by some party during election time."

But on the other side of the issue, Arye (Lova) Eliav, Labor's highly respected but not very influential dove, has said that if generals, even retired ones, went into politics, Israel would "become like the South American countries." General Rehavam Ze'evi, a member of the General Staff, has labelled the quick movement of generals into politics "undemocratic," calling for a "cooling-down" period of at least a year. "Commanders surrounded by the aura of leadership in the army," he has remarked, "should not expect this to accompany them immediately into political life. I regret to have to say that this has been a mistake made by both the Establishment and by the Opposition." And a retired senior officer who has asked that he not be identified told me that "this buisness of the Chief of Staff going directly into politics at the highest levels is very dangerous."

What does General Bar-Lev think of such criticism? In his first interview with an Israeli daily newspaper since he became a Minister he told the *Jerusalem Post*'s Mark Segal in March 1972:

> The question to be asked is whether or not a Cabinet post can be reached only through party politics. If the reply is in the affirmative, then Israel must accept that its leadership potential in the I.D.F. will be excluded from the top civilian positions. I realize that the example of Moshe Dayan is being quoted in this context, and how it took two years between his leaving the Army and entering politics, but that was 16 years ago, and things have changed since then.

> If I had been told—go into the party branch and work there, and in one-and-three-quarter years' time we will offer you a job, then my answer would have been to talk to me about it then. I would have looked for a serious job instead.

This has to be kept in mind if you do not wish to exclude persons like myself from the leadership.

While he didn't think it was right for politicians to approach soldiers when they were still in uniform, he didn't say it was downright wrong either, pointing out that one couldn't really expect soldiers not to plan for their after-Army lives. And as for the "politicization of the Army" as a result of what he and other retired generals were doing, he called such fears "imaginary."

What does the Israeli public think about generals in politics, according to the country's leading survey research organizations? In January 1970 PORI asked Israelis: "Was it right or wrong that political negotiations were held with General Ezer Weizman on his joining the Cabinet as a Minister before he resigned from the Army?" Forty percent said it was "right," thirteen percent said it was "somewhat wrong," seven percent said it was "wrong," thirty-six percent had no opinion, and almost four percent didn't answer. In November 1971 the Dahaf public opinion poll reported that forty-three percent of the population had no reservations whatsoever about senior officers entering politics, including the Cabinet. Thirty-three percent made their approval conditional upon the qualifications of the officers. About fourteen percent were somewhat against it, while 3.4 percent were very much against it. Presumably, the rest of those polled didn't answer or had no opinion. In December, 1971 PORI asked the public: "Was it right or wrong that it was announced that Haim Bar-Lev will receive a Cabinet Minister post before he ended his duty as Chief of Staff?" Forty-two percent answered "right," over seventeen percent answered "somewhat wrong," over twenty percent answered "wrong," and the rest either didn't answer or had no opinion. In that same week, when PORI asked: "Are you for or against handing Israeli's Ambassador to the U.S. Yitzchak Rabin a Cabinet Minister post?," it got the following results. Almost seventy-two percent said "for," twelve percent said "against," 1.4 percent said they "don't care," and the rest didn't know or didn't answer. (Incidentally, when Dahaf asked the same question in the Summer of 1973, when General Rabin had ended his tour as Israel's Ambassador to the United States, Rabin was still popular but somewhat less so. Sixty-one percent wanted him in the Cabinet, ten percent didn't, 23.5 percent were undecided, and 3.5 percent *didn't know who he was!*) In January 1972 PORI found that almost forty-eight percent of the public could not imagine a replacement for Moshe Dayan as the nation's Defense Minister. Finally, when in February 1973, PORI asked: "Is it or isn't it advisable that ex-generals should run on political tickets to the Knesset?," Fifty-four percent answered "advisable," over fifteen percent said that it "depends who" is running, almost twenty-one percent thought it "inadvisable," and the remaining ten percent were silent or without an opinion.

In sum, more and more retired military officers have "discovered" politics as their second career. What this infusion of generals and colonels into Israel's Knesset and Cabinet will untimately mean to the future relationship between the country's civilian and military leadership groups only the slow unfolding of time will reveal.

12

The "New Militarism"?: Or How Democratic Is a Democratic Garrison State?

A GARRISON STATE is an externally threatened state that is ruled by the military or strongly influenced by it. But Israel is a democratic garrison state. How democratic *is* a democratic garrison state? Isn't such a concept a contradiction that defies both logic and fact? And if it isn't—if a country can indeed be heavily militarized and dedicated to democratic values at the same time—is Israel a true example of such a country? Or have the Israelis simply invented a new kind of militarism, deluding themselves and deceiving others?

After all, the senior officer corps is honored, almost idolized. "Kol hakavod le'Zahal [All honor to the Army]," is a popular saying among Israelis. Zahal's retirees dominate much of the top and middle management of civilian Israel. More ex-generals and colonels are going into politics than ever before. The Army administers thousands of square miles of conquered territory and about a million conquered people. It censors the news media. It detains and deports individuals under Emergency

Regulations that are not subject to civilian judicial review. It takes the lion's share of the government's budget and gobbles up the nation's tax revenues. It influences basic economic and fiscal policies. It controls the weapons and aircraft industries. It is involved in religious questions. It has its own educational facilities. And it plays a commanding role in absorbing new immigrants and integrating old ones into the melting pot (or should one say the pressure cooker) of Israel. How is it therefore possible for such an institution *not* to eat away at the fabric and future of Israeli democracy?

It is possible because the words "military" and "militarized" are not synonyms for the word "militaristic." Discipline is not an antonym for democracy. There is no physically or psychologically isolated military elite: Zahal really is composed of soldiers who are on leave eleven months of the year, and the regular Army constantly interacts with the Reserves. It is possible because when the Cabinet decided to celebrate Israel's twenty-fifth anniversary with a massive military parade in Jerusalem in 1973, Defense Minister Dayan was a minority of one against it. So was the Army high command, which has always shunned such displays. It is possible because political and strategic opinion within the officer corps ranges from super-hawk to super-dove. Or as Ambassador Yitzchak Rabin, with not too much exaggeration, told a group of the American Professors for Peace in the Middle East in 1968: "In Israel most of the poets are hawks and most of the generals are doves."

It is possible because the Israeli General Staff takes its orders from the government; it does not give orders to the government. The 1956 and 1967 Arab-Israeli wars were begun—if by begun we mean who fired the first shot—by the Israeli Army. If the Army did not mount a pre-emptive strike in the 1973 Yom Kippur War, it was because the government ordered the Army not to do so. It is possible because Israelis, even as they fight, worry and talk about what such fighting is doing or may do to them as human beings. They are constantly expressing determination not to let the Sparta within them overwhelm the Athens within them, not to let the Garrison destroy the Democracy in their oh!-so-tiny Democratic Garrison State.

Right after the Six Day War a group of young kibbutz members recorded on tape the impressions of other kibbutz members about the war. The tapes were edited and published in a book which became an immediate bestseller. The English edition is called *The Seventh Day: Soldiers Talk About the Six Day War.* Coursing all through the discussions is the hope that Arab hatred of Israelis won't turn Israelis into militarists and haters of Arabs. As one of the Kibbutzniks, the father of seven children and the principal of a regional kibbutz high school, put it: "The big problem is one of education. How—despite the fact that from our point of view this was just a war—are we going to avoid turning into militarists?"

So long as he and others, including the professional fulltime officers who cannot return to their kibbutz between wars, worry about militarism—for just so long and no longer will Israel avoid it.

True, Zahal is more politicized than its officer corps cares to admit or than its general population realizes. But it is not— nor is it likely to become—so politicized as to threaten Israel's basic commitment to democracy. If there are deficiencies in Israeli democracy, they are not caused by the power or prestige of the Army. The multiplicity of political parties, the reliance on coalition government to form a Cabinet, the selection of Knesset candidates by a tiny group of party leaders and not by the voters, the failure to divide the country into many electoral constituencies so that the elected Knesset member has no particular interest in the voters and what they think between elections, the use of proportional representation to an absurd extreme, the self-perpetuation of aging political elites, and a bureaucracy that is as bloated as it is blasé and inefficient—all of these things are not due to the existence of the Army, its leaders, or its mission. They are the creation of those civilians who built Israel and those civilians who govern her.

The best answer I know to the questions "Is Israel's a new kind of militarism?" and "How democratic is her democratic garrison state?" was given to me by one of Israel's most important military officers, when we discussed them for hours and hours at the Israeli Pentagon in Tel-Aviv. "If I give my men orders," he said, "to march to Cairo, they will follow me blindly. But if I tell them to march on the Knesset, they'll just stand there and laugh at me."

APPENDICES

Appendix 1

Questions Asked of People Interviewed

1. How successful has Israel been in "demilitarizing" her armed forces and in maintaining civilian supremacy?
2. What is the overall influence of the Israel Defense Forces on the educational, economic, social, political, and administrative life of the country?
3. Is the high prestige of the IDF detrimental to non-military pursuits?
4. What happens to ranking officers when they leave the IDF?
5. How many retired IDF officers have been and are high and middle level officials in the Israeli civil service and quasi-governmental bodies like the Ports Authority, the Jewish Agency, the universities, etc.?
6. How many retired IDF officers have been and are in high and middle level positions in Israeli private firms?
7. How many of them have been or are in the Knesset?
8. How many of them are now or have been in the Cabinet?
9. How many active duty personnel study at the universities, and what do they study and what is their rank?

10. How many retired IDF officers become university teachers or administrators?
11. How many retired IDF officers go to work as civilians in the Ministry of Defense and in defense industries?
12. How many Israeli civilian workers work directly or indirectly for the IDF, the Ministry of Defense, and the defense industries?
13. What plans are the military and civilian authorities in Israel making for the eventual reconversion from war and semi-war to peace?
14. Are any of these plans completed and are they available?
15. What material has the IDF publishing house put out that is related to any of the above questions?
16. What does the military, in its publications, training, indoctrination, and educational programs, do *specifically* to inculcate in all ranks the principle of civilian control of the military institution?
17. Does the great need for and the prestige of the IDF in any way limit the kinds of public criticism and public checks of the military that one would ordinarily expect in a democracy?
18. Will the continued absence of real peace eventually destroy or weaken civilian supremacy in Israel?
19. What steps does the IDF take to eliminate or lessen political activity in the ranks?
20. Should Israel "worry" about "militarism"? If yes, why? If no, why not?
21. Is there another institution that matches the military in prestige and in its reputation for efficiency and service? If yes, which is it? If no, which one could or should Israel try to make into such a "rival" institution, and how should she go about it?

Appendix 2

The Proposed
1973/1974 Israeli Budget

Source: *Jerusalem Post,* January 9, 1973, p. 6.

Where the funds will come from

REVENUE
(In millions of IL)

	Estimate for 1973/74	Estimate for 1972/73	Actual Revenue 1971/72
TOTAL REVENUE	19,800	17,815	14,481
ORDINARY REVENUE	15,130	12,892	9,301
Revenue from loans and capital accounts	4,670	4,929	5,179
Ordinary revenue	15,130	12,892	9,301
Taxes and fees	12,900	10,715	8,557
Income & property tax	4,581	3,925	3,111
Income tax & defence levy	4,174	3,600	2,877
Property betterment tax	88	74	36
Property tax	319	251	198
Customs & surcharges	3,125	2,645	1,965
Purchase tax	1,696	1,258	921
Excise tax	362	310	262
Fuel tax	580	500	417
Travel tax	110	86	69
Revenue stamp tax	305	227	165
Entertainment tax	4	3	2
Defence stamp	240	191	147
Vehicle licences	70	57	50
Other licences and fees	186	167	119
Compulsory loans & Arnona	1,469	1,210	1,201
Savings loan	710	580	632
Defence loan	689	565	497
Arnona fund	70	65	71
Transferred revenues	516	365	260

APPENDIX 2

	REVENUE (In millions of IL)		
	Estimate for 1973/74	Estimate for 1972/73	Actual Revenue 1971/72
Interest & profits	623	572	535
Interest from loans	360	325	341
Interest from Government services	163	139	70
Interest from Government companies	22	22	20
Profits of Bank of Israel	70	80	101
Royalties	131	92	86
Miscellaneous revenues	97	159	121
Revenue from loans and capital accounts	4,670	4,929	5,179
Income from Government investments and loans	464	528	410
Revenue on a/c of participation in investment in communications	92	48	85
Revenues from State Lands Administration	29	22	45
Receipts on a/c pensions and compensations	77	61	55
National Insurance Institute Loan	830	820	647
Local bank loans	1,400	1,558	926
Foreign food surpluses	210	210	213
Foreign loans	3,066	2,196	2,275
Advance from Bank of Israel	—	650	650
Non-recurring items	—	252	—

And how they will be spent

	EXPENDITURE (In millions of IL)		
	Budget for 1973/74	Budget for 1972/73	Budget for 1971/72
TOTAL EXPENDITURE	19,800	17,815	14,338
ORDINARY EXPENDITURE	15,130	12,892	10,904
Development and capital expenditure	4,670	4,923	3,434
Ordinary expenditure	15,130	12,892	10,904
Administrative services	954	774	629
Presidency	1	1	1
Knesset	14	9	8
Cabinet Ministers	1	0.9	0.7
Prime Minister's Office	34	39	23
Finance Ministry	166	132	114
Interior Ministry	39	26	20

EXPENDITURE
(In millions of IL)

	Budget for 1973/74	Budget for 1972/73	Budget for 1971/72
Police Ministry	264	205	183
Justice Ministry	142	115	105
Foreign Affairs Ministry	62	46	35
State Comptroller	16	12	9
Retirement and compensations funds	154	118	108
Miscellaneous expenditure	25	65	17
Defence Ministry	6,065	5,458	5,546
Local authorities	671	520	428
Transferred expenditure to local authorities	516	365	260
Grants to local authorities	155	155	167
Social services	3,175	2,223	2,043
Min. of Education and Culture	1,433	995	816
Participation in Broadcasting Authority	3	2	15
Religious Affairs Ministry	38	30	33
Labour Ministry	90	74	64
Health Ministry	443	270	295
Disability compensations	96	66	61
Social Welfare Ministry	163	107	100
National Insurance Institute	220	190	171
Housing Ministry	52	24	12
Absorption Ministry	35	24	21
Price subsidies	600	437	451
Economic Services	1,448	1,281	1,102
Agriculture Ministry	82	64	63
Development Min.	33	9	12
Atomic Energy Commission	59	56	51
Commerce & Industry Min.	135	97	59
Tourism Ministry	37	31	17
Export incentives	950	910	797
Transport Ministry	49	42	27
Participation in Railways budget	24	19	23
Contribution and rebates for transport	24	11	13
Public Works Dept. and land surveys	53	38	35
Interest payments	2,000	1,740	1,151
Reserves	814	893	1.9
Special budgets	700	803	1.4
Development & Capital expenditure	4,670	4,923	3,434
Development expenditure	2,501	2,251	2,275

EXPENDITURE
(In millions of IL)

	Budget for 1973/74	Budget for 1972/73	Budget for 1971/72
Administrative Services	39	21	12
Government buildings	15	9	6
Police and prisons	21	8	4
Courts	2	3	1
Local authorities	74	52	37
Social services	1,269	1,188	1,319
Education	70	77	54
Higher education	100	70	69
Religious	4	2	3
Employment and vocational training	19	13	6
Health	110	44	39
Social welfare	31	11	4
Housing	934	969	1,142
Economic sector	1,118	989	905
Agriculture	79	76	122
Waterworks	60	52	53
Quarries, mines and electricity	25	23	39
Oil lines and drilling	10	5	11
Manufacturing	285	277	209
Tourism	40	30	22
Transport	151	117	108
Roads	103	81	65
Communications	330	304	240
Miscellaneous investments in enterprises	35	19	32
Debt repayments	2,028	2,125	1,138
Budgetary revolving fund	40	200	21
Reserve for development expenditure	100	94	—
Non-recurring items	—	252	—

Appendix 3

Some Public Opinion Surveys of Israelis' Attitudes Toward Their Army

Source: Printed by permission of PORI, Public Opinion Research of Israel Ltd.

APPENDIX 3

Do you justify or not the evacuation of the Bedouins from the Rafiah Area?
(asked May 14-17, 1972)

	Justify	Un-justify	Never heard of it	D.K.		(N)
ALL	62.0	30.2	6.9	1.0	100.0	1206
BY SEX						
Male	69.2	24.1	5.7	1.0	100.0	603
Female	53.7	37.1	8.3	0.9	100.0	603
BY AGE						
18-29	56.7	38.8	4.5	0.0	100.0	351
30-39	58.3	33.3	7.3	1.0	100.0	239
40-49	68.1	27.5	3.8	0.5	100.0	252
50-59	70.7	20.7	6.4	2.1	100.0	189
60 and Over	62.5	20.8	15.0	1.7	100.0	170
BY EDUCATION						
College	65.9	27.1	6.6	0.4	100.0	295
High School	62.6	31.7	4.8	1.0	100.0	503
Grade School & Less	58.1	30.6	10.0	1.3	100.0	408
BY OCCUPATION						
Manual	62.4	30.2	6.7	0.7	100.0	361
White Collar & Business	59.7	34.5	5.8	0.0	100.0	188
Professional	75.5	19.7	4.1	0.7	100.0	188
Not in Working Force	56.7	32.8	8.7	1.7	100.0	469
BY INCOME						
Above Average	72.2	22.9	4.9	0.0	100.0	370
Average	61.1	34.1	4.8	0.0	100.0	385
Below Average	54.8	33.4	9.3	2.4	100.0	396
FATHER'S COUNTRY BY BIRTH						
Europe, America	65.7	26.6	6.7	1.0	100.0	665
Asia, Africa	59.2	33.7	6.6	0.5	100.0	491
BY SENIORITY IN COUNTRY						
Israeli born	62.8	28.6	7.3	1.3	100.0	286
Immigrated through 1947	68.4	25.3	4.7	1.6	100.0	262
Immigrated 1948-1952	57.7	34.6	6.7	1.0	100.0	406
Immigrated 1953 or later	61.5	29.7	8.9	0.0	100.0	252

PORI, Public Opinion Research of Israel Ltd. Study 215. I.D. 14-17/5, 1972.

**Should or shouldn't the name of the high-ranking officer
who was censured by the General Staff on the
Rafiah Bedouins' evacuation be disclosed?**
(asked May 14-17, 1972)

	Should	Shouldn't	D.K.	N.A.		(N)
ALL	15.6	65.1	18.4	0.9	100.0	1206
BY SEX						
Male	15.3	71.7	12.1	0.8	100.0	603
Female	16.0	58.4	24.6	1.0	100.0	603
BY AGE						
18-29	18.9	69.1	11.7	0.3	100.0	351
30-39	17.7	62.0	19.8	0.4	100.0	239
40-49	13.5	67.9	17.5	1.2	100.0	252
50-59	14.8	66.1	16.9	2.1	100.0	189
60 and Over	10.0	55.9	33.5	0.6	100.0	170
BY EDUCATION						
College	16.6	72.2	10.8	0.3	100.0	295
High School	16.4	69.9	13.0	0.8	100.0	503
Grade School & Less	14.0	53.9	30.5	1.5	100.0	408
BY OCCUPATION						
Manual	17.0	65.5	16.2	1.4	100.0	361
White Collar & Business	17.2	72.6	9.7	0.5	100.0	188
Professional	14.4	78.7	6.9	0.0	100.0	188
Not in Working Force	14.5	56.3	28.1	1.1	100.0	469
BY INCOME						
Above Average	15.1	77.6	7.3	0.0	100.0	370
Average	15.9	70.0	12.8	1.3	100.0	385
Below Average	14.7	52.5	32.0	0.8	100.0	396
FATHER'S COUNTRY OF BIRTH						
Europe, America	13.5	69.7	16.2	0.6	100.0	665
Asia, Africa	19.6	57.4	21.8	1.2	100.0	491
BY SENIORITY IN COUNTRY						
Israeli Born	15.1	72.5	10.9	1.4	100.0	286
Immigrated through 1947	18.7	64.1	16.8	0.4	100.0	262
Immigrated 1948-1952	15.6	62.6	21.3	0.5	100.0	406
Immigrated 1953 or later	13.1	61.5	23.8	1.6	100.0	252

PORI, Public Opinion Research of Israel Ltd. Study 215. I.D. 14-17/5, 1972.

Who in your opinion will lead the country in a hundred years' time?

(asked October 4-9, 1972)

	No one of those	D.K.	TV people	Philosophers	Pollsters	Economists	Scientists	Computer experts	Jurists	Politicians	Army officers	N.A.		(N)
ALL	4.2	31.4	0.3	1.2	0.6	2.1	12.8	7.1	0.8	26.0	12.6	0.7	100.0	1234
BY SEX														
Male	3.4	28.2	0.5	2.1	0.3	2.1	13.8	6.2	0.8	28.2	13.3	1.1	100.0	617
Female	5.0	34.7	0.2	0.3	1.0	2.1	11.8	7.9	0.8	23.8	12.0	0.3	100.0	617
BY AGE														
18-29	6.4	23.3	0.9	1.5	0.0	1.5	12.1	8.2	0.9	28.8	15.8	0.6	100.0	330
30-39	3.2	26.7	0.0	2.0	0.0	2.8	11.2	9.6	0.4	30.3	13.1	0.8	100.0	251
40-49	3.5	34.6	0.4	0.4	2.7	2.3	10.9	4.7	0.8	25.3	14.0	0.4	100.0	257
50-59	4.6	34.2	0.0	0.5	0.0	3.1	18.9	6.6	1.0	21.9	9.2	0.0	100.0	196
60 and Over	2.5	44.0	0.0	1.5	0.5	1.0	12.5	5.5	1.0	21.0	8.5	2.0	100.0	200
BY EDUCATION														
College	4.8	21.7	0.0	0.7	0.0	3.4	13.1	7.9	0.7	37.2	8.6	1.7	100.0	290
High School	3.9	27.5	0.7	1.7	0.9	2.4	13.6	9.9	1.3	25.1	12.5	0.6	100.0	545
Grade School & Less	4.3	43.9	0.0	1.0	0.8	0.8	11.5	2.5	0.3	19.0	15.8	0.3	100.0	399
BY OCCUPATION														
Manual	3.7	31.4	0.0	1.7	0.8	2.3	13.6	5.4	1.4	22.6	16.9	0.3	100.0	354
White Collar & Business	5.2	28.0	0.9	0.5	1.4	1.9	14.2	9.5	0.9	25.1	10.9	1.4	100.0	211
Professional	4.5	22.8	0.0	1.5	0.0	4.0	13.4	8.4	0.0	39.6	5.4	0.5	100.0	202
Not in Working Force	4.1	36.8	0.4	1.1	0.4	1.3	11.3	6.6	0.6	23.1	13.3	0.9	100.0	467
BY INCOME														
Above Average	2.2	23.1	0.5	1.2	1.0	3.2	13.9	8.7	0.7	35.5	9.4	0.5	100.0	403
Average	4.8	30.1	0.0	0.6	0.3	1.8	13.7	10.4	1.2	21.8	14.6	0.6	100.0	335
Below Average	4.6	37.6	0.5	1.9	0.7	1.6	10.0	3.7	0.7	22.3	15.5	0.9	100.0	431
FATHER'S COUNTRY OF BIRTH														
Europe, America	3.3	26.4	0.5	1.3	0.9	2.4	15.6	7.4	0.9	27.9	12.2	1.1	100.0	755
Asia, Africa	6.3	39.9	0.0	1.0	0.2	1.9	8.2	5.8	0.5	21.7	14.3	0.2	100.0	414
BY SENIORITY IN COUNTRY														
Israeli born	4.2	23.9	0.6	0.3	0.0	1.7	10.8	8.9	0.8	33.3	14.7	0.8	100.0	360
Immigrated through 1947	4.3	35.5	0.0	1.4	0.7	3.6	15.1	6.8	1.1	20.4	9.7	1.4	100.0	279
Immigrated 1948-1952	2.8	32.3	0.5	2.1	1.5	1.5	15.1	5.1	0.3	24.4	14.4	0.0	100.0	390
Immigrated 1953 or Later	5.9	38.1	0.0	1.0	0.0	2.0	8.4	7.9	1.5	24.3	9.9	1.0	100.0	202

PORI, Public Opinion Research of Israel Ltd. Study 225. I.D. 4-9/10, 1972.

Should or shouldn't there be a cut in the defense budget?
(asked October 28 - November 3, 1971)

	Should	Shouldn't	D.K.	N.A.		(N)
ALL	21.1	61.9	16.0	0.9	100.0	1201
BY SEX						
Male	25.9	59.8	13.8	0.5	100.0	587
Female	16.5	64.4	17.8	1.3	100.0	607
BY AGE						
18-29	27.6	58.4	13.4	0.6	100.0	351
30-39	23.3	61.3	15.0	0.4	100.0	266
40-49	16.9	65.2	15.9	2.0	100.0	201
50-59	16.2	65.9	16.8	1.1	100.0	179
60 and Over	15.9	61.7	21.4	1.0	100.0	201
BY EDUCATION						
College	18.2	61.0	19.3	1.5	100.0	269
High School	19.9	67.3	12.0	0.8	100.0	502
Grade School & Less	24.7	55.8	18.8	0.7	100.0	425
BY OCCUPATION						
Manual	24.8	63.5	11.4	0.3	100.0	359
White Collar & Business	26.9	60.1	11.1	1.9	100.0	208
Professional	15.4	63.5	21.2	0.0	100.0	156
Not in Working Force	17.8	61.0	19.9	1.3	100.0	477
BY INCOME						
Above Average	22.2	62.3	14.5	0.9	100.0	324
Average	20.8	64.5	13.3	1.4	100.0	361
Below Average	20.8	60.0	18.6	0.6	100.0	462
FATHER'S COUNTRY OF BIRTH						
Europe, America	17.6	66.9	14.4	1.1	100.0	703
Asia, Africa	26.2	55.2	18.0	0.7	100.0	451
BY SENIORITY IN COUNTRY						
Israeli born	23.4	62.8	12.8	1.0	100.0	290
Immigrated through 1947	20.9	60.7	17.2	1.3	100.0	239
Immigrated 1948-1952	18.0	65.0	17.0	0.0	100.0	423
Immigrated 1953 or Later	23.2	57.7	17.1	2.0	100.0	246

PORI, Public Opinion Research of Israel Ltd. Study 202. I.D. 28/10-3/11, 1971.

APPENDIX 3

In your opinion does the Government spend too much, too little, or just what is needed on defense?

(asked December 7-12, 1971)

	Too much	Too little	Just right	D.K.	N.A.		(N)
ALL	8.6	12.5	65.3	11.5	2.0	100.0	1205
BY SEX							
Male	10.3	14.4	64.7	9.0	1.7	100.0	592
Female	7.0	10.8	65.9	14.0	2.3	100.0	613
BY AGE							
18-29	14.8	9.8	65.2	8.6	1.5	100.0	325
30-39	9.6	7.9	71.9	8.3	2.2	100.0	228
40-49	6.0	15.9	62.5	12.4	3.2	100.0	251
50-59	5.5	14.6	62.3	16.6	1.0	100.0	199
60 and Over	4.0	15.8	64.4	13.9	2.0	100.0	202
BY EDUCATION							
College	10.2	12.2	65.0	11.2	1.4	100.0	294
High School	10.4	12.5	65.2	10.4	1.5	100.0	463
Grade School & Less	5.9	12.8	65.5	12.8	2.9	100.0	444
BY OCCUPATION							
Manual	8.8	13.8	64.1	11.6	1.9	100.0	320
White Collar & Business	7.7	17.4	62.6	10.8	1.5	100.0	195
Professional	11.9	11.9	62.7	10.4	3.1	100.0	193
Not in Working Force	7.6	10.1	68.2	12.3	1.8	100.0	497
BY INCOME							
Above Average	9.2	12.9	66.5	9.9	1.5	100.0	272
Average	7.7	13.4	68.2	8.5	2.2	100.0	365
Below Average	9.2	10.7	63.3	14.4	2.3	100.0	521
FATHER'S COUNTRY OF BIRTH							
Europe, America	6.6	13.7	65.8	12.6	1.3	100.0	685
Asia, Africa	10.9	11.3	64.3	10.7	2.8	100.0	468
BY SENIORITY IN COUNTRY							
Israeli born	12.0	10.3	66.7	9.3	1.7	100.0	291
Immigrated through 1947	3.0	13.1	65.7	15.3	3.0	100.0	236
Immigrated 1948-1952	9.5	12.4	67.6	8.6	1.8	100.0	442
Immigrated 1953 or Later	8.1	14.9	59.1	16.2	1.7	100.0	235

PORI, Public Opinion Research of Israel Ltd. Study 205. I.D. 7-12/12, 1971.

What is your opinion about enlisting yeshivot [Talmudic seminary] students? Should they serve in the Army as any other young man, enlist for a short period only, or not serve at all?

(asked August 16-22, 1972)

	Serve at all	Short period	Not serve at all	D.K.	N.A.		(N)
ALL	81.9	10.6	3.5	2.2	1.9	100.0	1206
BY SEX							
Male	81.0	13.8	3.5	1.5	0.2	100.0	598
Female	82.9	7.3	3.4	2.9	3.4	100.0	605
BY AGE							
18-29	81.3	11.8	4.3	1.7	0.9	100.0	355
30-39	81.4	9.9	4.2	2.3	2.3	100.0	266
40-49	85.0	9.9	1.7	2.6	0.9	100.0	241
50-59	81.3	12.5	3.4	1.7	1.1	100.0	181
60 and Over	85.0	8.2	3.4	3.4	0.0	100.0	147
BY EDUCATION							
College	75.8	15.1	7.2	1.1	0.8	100.0	270
High School	86.9	9.1	2.1	1.3	0.6	100.0	543
Grade School & Less	79.1	9.4	2.9	4.2	4.5	100.0	393
BY OCCUPATION							
Manual	86.8	10.7	0.9	·0.6	0.9	100.0	322
White Collar & Business	82.0	10.5	4.2	2.1	1.3	100.0	243
Professional	75.3	16.9	6.6	0.6	0.6	100.0	174
Not in Working Force	80.8	8.3	3.7	3.9	3.3	100.0	467
BY INCOME							
Above Average	82.3	10.9	3.8	1.2	1.8	100.0	347
Average	82.6	12.8	2.5	1.5	0.5	100.0	408
Below Average	83.0	8.2	4.1	3.1	1.5	100.0	390
FATHER'S COUNTRY OF BIRTH							
Europe, America	83.0	10.2	3.9	1.5	1.5	100.0	694
Asia, Africa	81.2	12.0	3.1	3.3	0.5	100.0	433
BY SENIORITY IN COUNTRY							
Israeli born	82.9	8.5	3.5	1.3	3.8	100.0	334
Immigrated through 1947	81.0	13.1	4.4	0.4	1.2	100.0	255
Immigrated 1948-1952	82.9	11.3	2.3	2.5	1.0	100.0	400
Immigrated 1953 or Later	79.6	9.3	4.6	5.1	1.4	100.0	216

PORI, Public Opinion Research of Israel Ltd. Study 220. I.D. 16-22/8, 1972.

APPENDIX 3

What is your opinion on religious girls' enlistment? Are you for enlisting religious girls for regular Army service, against regular Army service but for national civil service, or do you think a religious girl should not leave her home at all?

(asked January 23-27, 1972)

	Regular army service	Civil service	Oppose any service	D.K.	N.A.		(N)
ALL	52.0	29.6	14.0	4.1	0.3	100.0	1181
BY SEX							
Male	51.3	32.5	11.9	4.1	0.2	100.0	581
Female	52.7	26.8	16.0	4.0	0.5	100.0	600
BY AGE							
18-29	53.2	26.7	17.1	2.1	0.8	100.0	374
30-39	50.5	35.4	10.1	4.0	0.0	100.0	277
40-49	47.0	34.3	14.4	3.8	0.4	100.0	236
50-59	59.3	22.8	12.6	5.4	0.0	100.0	167
60 and Over	48.8	27.3	14.9	9.1	0.0	100.0	121
BY EDUCATION							
College	49.7	35.0	12.6	2.8	0.0	100.0	286
High School	54.5	30.8	9.6	4.4	0.8	100.0	481
Grade School & Less	50.7	24.6	20.0	4.6	0.0	100.0	414
BY OCCUPATION							
Manual	53.4	28.9	12.1	5.3	0.3	100.0	339
White Collar & Business	52.5	31.9	13.7	2.0	0.0	100.0	204
Professional	58.3	35.0	3.9	1.7	1.1	100.0	180
Not in Working Force	48.3	27.1	19.4	5.0	0.2	100.0	458
BY INCOME							
Above Average	55.6	34.4	6.9	3.1	0.0	100.0	320
Average	54.8	31.4	8.5	4.1	1.1	100.0	363
Below Average	43.6	28.8	23.6	4.0	0.0	100.0	420
FATHER'S COUNTRY OF BIRTH							
Europe, America	54.2	31.8	9.2	4.2	0.6	100.0	686
Asia, Africa	47.1	27.6	21.1	4.2	0.0	100.0	431
BY SENIORITY IN COUNTRY							
Israeli born	56.0	29.1	12.7	1.9	0.3	100.0	316
Immigrated through 1947	57.4	28.2	8.5	5.3	0.5	100.0	188
Immigrated 1948-1952	45.5	33.4	17.5	3.1	0.5	100.0	422
Immigrated 1953 or Later	53.7	25.1	13.7	7.5	0.0	100.0	255

PORI, Public Opinion Research of Israel Ltd. Study 208. I.D. 23-27/1, 1972.

Was it right or wrong that political negotiations were held with General Ezer Weizman on his joining the Cabinet as a Minister before he resigned from the Army?

(asked during January, 1970)

	Right	Somewhat wrong	Wrong	D.K.	N.A.	
ALL	40.0	13.1	7.2	35.9	3.6	100.0
BY SEX						
Male	41.5	12.8	10.3	28.2	6.9	100.0
Female	38.4	13.3	4.6	42.6	0.8	100.0
BY AGE						
14-17	54.5	13.6	9.0	22.7	0.0	100.0
18-19	46.1	7.6	15.3	30.7	0.0	100.0
20-29	45.7	19.1	7.4	24.4	3.1	100.0
30-39	42.7	14.5	5.2	37.5	0.0	100.0
40-49	31.7	13.4	12.1	41.4	1.2	100.0
50-59	37.7	9.8	3.2	40.9	8.1	100.0
60-69	36.5	7.6	7.6	44.2	3.8	100.0
70 and Over	33.3	6.6	0.0	53.3	6.6	100.0
BY OCCUPATION						
Housewives	33.8	11.5	3.5	49.6	1.4	100.0
Services	20.5	23.0	12.8	43.5	0.0	100.0
Blue Collar	41.6	8.3	11.6	33.3	5.0	100.0
Transport, Communication	58.8	17.6	5.8	17.6	0.0	100.0
Sales Workers	54.5	9.0	0.0	18.1	18.1	100.0
Clerical	36.5	15.3	11.5	32.6	3.8	100.0
Professional	50.8	15.2	10.1	23.7	0.0	100.0
Don't Work	52.4	11.4	3.2	27.8	4.9	100.0
BY DISTRICT						
Jerusalem	48.7	21.9	4.8	24.3	0.0	100.0
North	24.3	17.0	2.4	51.2	4.8	100.0
Haifa	51.7	10.7	5.3	25.0	7.1	100.0
Center	33.0	18.0	11.0	34.0	4.0	100.0
Tel Aviv	43.3	8.2	7.6	38.2	2.5	100.0
South	35.5	11.1	4.4	44.4	4.4	100.0

PORI, Public Opinion Research of Israel Ltd. Study 181. I.D. Jan. 1970.

Was it right or wrong that it was announced that
Haim Bar-Lev will receive a Cabinet Minister's post
before he ended his duty as Chief of Staff?

(asked December 7-12, 1971)

	Right	Somewhat wrong	Wrong	D.K.	N.A.		(N)
ALL	42.0	17.7	20.7	18.7	0.9	100.0	1205
BY SEX							
Male	43.1	18.6	24.0	12.8	1.5	100.0	592
Female	40.9	16.8	17.6	24.3	0.3	100.0	613
BY AGE							
18-29	42.8	20.3	22.5	14.5	0.0	100.0	325
30-39	41.7	15.8	21.1	20.6	0.9	100.0	228
40-49	45.0	19.5	17.5	17.1	0.8	100.0	251
50-59	41.7	17.6	20.6	19.6	0.5	100.0	199
60 and Over	37.6	13.4	21.8	24.3	3.0	100.0	202
BY EDUCATION							
College	41.2	15.6	29.3	12.6	1.4	100.0	294
High School	42.8	20.3	21.6	15.3	0.0	100.0	463
Grade School & Less	41.9	16.2	14.4	25.9	1.6	100.0	444
BY OCCUPATION							
Manual	39.4	19.7	21.3	19.7	0.0	100.0	320
White Collar & Business	49.2	15.4	22.1	12.3	1.0	100.0	195
Professional	39.4	18.7	30.6	10.4	1.0	100.0	193
Not in Working Force	41.9	16.9	16.1	23.7	1.4	100.0	497
BY INCOME							
Above Average	42.6	16.2	31.6	8.1	1.5	100.0	272
Average	41.4	19.2	21.1	18.4	0.0	100.0	365
Below Average	41.7	18.6	16.1	23.4	0.2	100.0	521
FATHER'S COUNTRY OF BIRTH							
Europe, America	41.5	17.7	22.6	17.8	0.4	100.0	685
Asia, Africa	42.1	18.6	18.8	20.3	0.2	100.0	468
BY SENIORITY IN COUNTRY							
Israeli born	40.5	21.0	22.7	13.4	2.4	100.0	291
Immigrated through 1947	41.1	11.9	29.7	16.1	1.3	100.0	236
Immigrated 1948-1952	42.1	20.8	19.7	17.2	0.2	100.0	442
Immigrated 1953 or Later	44.7	13.6	11.1	30.6	0.0	100.0	235

PORI, Public Opinion Research of Israel Ltd. Study 205. I.D. 7-12/12, 1971.

Are you for or against handing Israel's Ambassador to the U.S. Yitzchak Rabin a Cabinet Minister's post?

(asked December 7-12, 1972)

	For	Against	D.K.	Don't care	N.A.		(N)
ALL	71.7	12.1	13.6	1.4	1.2	100.0	1205
BY SEX							
Male	69.8	14.7	12.7	1.2	1.7	100.0	592
Female	73.6	9.6	14.5	1.6	0.7	100.0	613
BY AGE							
18-29	72.9	12.9	12.6	0.9	0.6	100.0	325
30-39	71.5	13.2	13.6	0.4	1.3	100.0	228
40-49	73.7	11.2	12.7	1.2	1.2	100.0	251
50-59	66.3	12.6	17.6	3.5	0.0	100.0	199
60 and Over	72.8	10.4	12.4	1.5	3.0	100.0	202
BY EDUCATION							
College	70.7	13.3	11.2	4.1	0.7	100.0	294
High School	72.4	11.9	14.5	0.2	1.1	100.0	463
Grade School & Less	71.6	11.7	14.2	0.9	1.6	100.0	444
BY OCCUPATION							
Manual	71.9	15.6	11.3	0.6	0.6	100.0	320
White Collar & Business	71.8	12.3	13.8	2.1	0.0	100.0	195
Professional	71.0	10.4	13.5	4.1	1.0	100.0	193
Not in Working Force	71.8	10.5	15.1	0.6	2.0	100.0	497
BY INCOME							
Above Average	72.8	10.7	11.8	3.7	1.1	100.0	272
Average	73.4	10.7	13.2	1.6	1.1	100.0	365
Below Average	71.8	14.0	13.8	0.2	0.2	100.0	521
FATHER'S COUNTRY OF BIRTH							
Europe, America	73.0	11.2	13.1	1.8	0.9	100.0	685
Asia, Africa	71.2	13.7	14.1	0.6	0.4	100.0	468
BY SENIORITY IN COUNTRY							
Israeli born	67.7	13.7	12.4	1.7	4.5	100.0	291
Immigrated through 1947	68.6	12.3	14.8	4.2	0.0	100.0	236
Immigrated 1948-1952	73.8	12.7	12.9	0.5	0.2	100.0	442
Immigrated 1953 or Later	76.2	8.5	15.3	0.0	0.0	100.0	235

PORI, Public Opinion Research of Israel Ltd. Study 205. I.D. 7-12/12, 1971.

Is it or isn't it advisable that ex-Army generals
should run on political tickets for the Knesset?

(asked February 11-15, 1973)

	Advisable	Depends who	Inad-visable	D.K.	N.A.		(N)
ALL	53.8	15.5	20.6	9.6	0.5	100.0	1203
BY SEX							
Male	53.2	16.2	25.1	5.1	0.3	100.0	593
Female	54.4	14.8	16.3	14.0	0.7	100.0	610
BY AGE							
18-29	53.6	19.1	20.8	6.3	0.3	100.0	353
30-39	54.6	12.0	28.3	5.2	0.0	100.0	254
40-49	52.3	20.5	15.0	11.4	0.9	100.0	222
50-59	53.8	12.6	16.5	16.5	0.5	100.0	182
60 and Over	55.0	10.5	20.4	13.1	1.0	100.0	192
BY EDUCATION							
College	48.2	22.9	22.2	6.3	0.4	100.0	285
High School	53.8	15.2	23.5	6.9	0.6	100.0	507
Grade School & Less	57.8	10.6	15.8	15.3	0.5	100.0	411
BY OCCUPATION							
Manual	59.7	12.0	18.5	9.2	0.6	100.0	326
White Collar & Business	53.3	19.0	23.3	4.3	0.0	100.0	211
Professional	48.3	21.3	24.2	6.3	0.0	100.0	207
Not in Working Force	52.3	13.7	19.2	13.9	0.9	100.0	459
BY INCOME							
Above Average	53.6	19.4	21.5	4.4	1.0	100.0	387
Average	56.9	12.2	24.7	6.3	0.0	100.0	288
Below Average	54.8	11.8	17.5	15.7	0.2	100.0	447
FATHER'S COUNTRY OF BIRTH							
Europe, America	49.8	20.0	20.2	9.4	0.6	100.0	641
Asia, Africa	58.0	10.0	21.6	10.0	0.4	100.0	497
BY SENIORITY IN COUNTRY							
Israeli born	56.4	18.8	20.1	4.8	0.0	100.0	318
Immigrated through 1947	52.8	18.3	20.0	7.2	1.7	100.0	235
Immigrated 1948-1952	55.3	9.9	20.7	13.6	0.5	100.0	436
Immigrated 1953 or Later	48.1	18.9	21.7	11.3	0.0	100.0	214

PORI, Public Opinion Research of Israel Ltd. Study 234. I.D. 11-15/2, 1973.

Selected Bibliography

I. Books, Government Publications, and Special Studies

Allon, Yigal. *The Making of Israel's Army.* London: Vallentine, Mitchell & Co. Ltd., 1970.

Axelrod, Laurence Wayne. "Zahal and Israeli Society: A Political and Sociological Analysis." Political Science Honors Paper, Temple University, 1971.

Ben-Shaul, Moshe (ed.). *Generals of Israel.* Tel-Aviv: Hadar Publishing Co., Ltd., 1968.

Bondy, Ruth, Ohad, Zmora, and Bashan, Raphael (eds.). *Mission Survival.* New York: Sabra Books, 1968.

Caiden, Gerald E. *Israel's Administrative Culture.* Berkeley: Institute of Governmental Studies of the University of California, 1970.

Foot, M. R. D. *Men in Uniform: Military Manpower in Modern Industrial Societies.* New York: Frederick A. Praeger, Publisher for the Institute of Strategic Studies of London, 1961.

Gates, David F. and Heymont, Irving. *An Exploratory Study of the Role of Armed Forces in Education: Iran, Israel, Peru, and Turkey.* McLean, Virginia: Research Analysis Corporation, 1968.

SELECTED BIBLIOGRAPHY

Glick, Edward Bernard. *Peaceful Conflict: The Non-Military Use of the Military.* Harrisburg, Pennsylvania: Stackpole Books, 1967.

Glick, Edward Bernard. *Soldiers, Scholars, and Society: The Social Impact of the American Military.* Pacific Palisades, California: Goodyear Publishing Company, Inc., 1971.

Hanning, Hugh. *The Peaceful Uses of Military Forces.* New York: Frederick A. Praeger, Publishers in cooperation with the World Veterans Federation, 1967.

Hurewitz, J. C. *Middle East Politics: The Military Dimension.* New York: Frederick A Praeger, Publishers for the Council on Foreign Relations, 1969.

Israel. *Chen.* Tel-Aviv: Ministry of Defence Publishing House, 1969.

Israel. *Facts about Israel.* Jerusalem: Ministry for Foreign Affairs, 1973.

Israel. *Gadna.* Tel-Aviv: Ministry of Defence Publishing House, 1970.

Israel. *Israel Government Year Book.* Jerusalem: Central Office of Information, 1962–.

Israel. *Nahal.* Tel-Aviv: Ministry of Defence Publishing House, 1970.

Israel. *Statistical Abstract of Israel.* Jerusalem: Central Bureau of Statistics, 1970 and 1972.

Kanovsky, Eliyahu. *The Economic Impact of the Six-Day War: Israel, the Occupied Territories, Egypt, Jordan.* New York: Praeger Publishers, 1970.

Near, Henry (ed.). *The Seventh Day: Soldiers' Talk about the Six-Day War.* Tel-Aviv: Steimatzky's Agency Ltd. in association with Andre Deutsch, 1970.

Peres, Shimon. *David's Sling: The Arming of Israel.* London: Weidenfeld and Nicolson, 1970.

Perlmutter, Amos. *Military and Politics in Israel: Nation-Building and Role Expansion.* New York: Frederick A. Praeger, Publishers, 1969.

Rolbant, Samuel. *The Israel Soldier: Profile of an Army.* New York: Thomas Yoseloff, 1970.

Teveth, Shabtai. *The Cursed Blessing: The Story of Israel's Occupation of the West Bank.* London: Weidenfeld and Nicolson, 1970.

Teveth, Shabtai. *Moshe Dayan*. Jerusalem: Steimatzky's Agency with Weidenfeld and Nicolson, 1972.

Zweig, Ferdynand. *Israel: The Sword and the Harp*. London: Heinemann Educational Books Ltd., 1969.

II. Articles

Artzyeli, Mordechai. "High School Seniors Thinking Out Loud," *Israel Magazine*, III (February 1971), 75-78.

Bar-On, Colonel Mordechai M. "Education Processes in the Israel Defense Forces," in Tax, Sol (ed.). *The Draft: A Handbook of Facts and Alternatives*. Chicago: The University of Chicago Press, 1967, pp. 138-166.

Dershowitz, Alan M. "Terrorism and Preventive Detention: The Case of Israel," *Commentary*, L (December 1970), 67-78.

Eaton, Joseph W. "Gadna: Israel's Youth Corps," *Middle East Journal*, XXIII (Autumn 1969), 471-483.

Elon, Amos. "The Mood: Self-Confidence and a Subdued Sadness," *The New York Times Magazine* (May 6, 1973), pp. 33ff.

Elon, Amos. "Two Arab Towns that Plumb Israel's Conscience," *The New York Times Magazine* (October 22, 1972), pp. 44ff.

Friedler, Ya'acov. "Revolt of the Druse," *The Jerusalem Post Magazine* (March 26, 1971), pp. 6-8.

"A General Takes Charge of 'Koor,'" *Histadrut Foto News*, XXV (November 1968), 4.

Glick, Edward Bernard. "'And the Builders Had Every One His Sword,'" *Jewish Frontier*, XXXV (March 1968), 17-19.

Glick, Edward Bernard. "The Draft and Nonmilitary National Service," *Military Review*, XLIX (December 1969), 86-90.

Glick, Edward Bernard. "The Nonmilitary Use of the Latin American Military," in Bailey, Norman A. (ed.). *Latin America: Politics, Economics, and Hemispheric Security*. New York: Frederick A. Praeger, Publishers for the Center of Strategic Studies of Georgetown University, 1965, pp. 179-191.

Glick, Edward Bernard. "The Nonmilitary Use of the Latin American Military: A More Realistic Approach to Arms Control and Disarmament," *Background* (since renamed *International Studies Quarterly*), VIII (November 1964), 161-173.

Glick, Edward Bernard. "Should We Eliminate or Merge Our Military Academies?," *Foreign Service Journal*, XLVIII (January 1971), 22ff.

SELECTED BIBLIOGRAPHY

Halpren, Ben. "The Role of the Military in Israel," in Johnson, John J. (ed.). *The Role of the Military in Underdeveloped Countries.* Princeton: Princeton University Press, 1962, pp. 317-357.

Heiman, Leo. "Is Israel a Military Nation?," *The Jewish Digest,* XV (August 1969), 53-55.

Heiman, Leo. "Israel's Nahal Corps," *Military Review,* XLVII (July 1967), 65-70.

Heymont, Irving. "The Israeli Career Officer Corps," *Military Review,* XLVIII (October 1968), 13-19.

Hirth, Paula. "The Women's Army Corps," *Israel Magazine,* III (February 1971), 31-46.

Hurewitz, J. C. "The Role of the Military in Society and Government in Israel," in Fisher, Sidney Nettleton (ed.). *The Military in the Middle East.* Columbus: Ohio State University Press, 1963, pp. 89-104.

Levenberg, Alisa. "Camp Marcus: Model School for Adults," *Pioneer Woman,* XL (January 1965), 7ff.

Lowenstein, Ralph L. "Military Press Censorship in Israel," *Military Review,* L (February 1970), 3-9.

Peled, Mattatyahu. "The Pressures of Waiting," *The Jerusalem Post Weekly* (June 9, 1969), pp. 7-8.

Radom, Matthew. "Military Officers and Business Leaders: An Israeli Study in Contrasts," *Columbia Journal of World Business,* III (March-April 1968), 27-34.

Raphaeli, Nimrod. "Military Government in the Occupied Territories: An Israeli View," *Middle East Journal,* XXIII (Spring 1969), 177-190.

Rothman, Rozann C. "Education and Participation in the Israeli Defence Forces," *Jewish Social Studies,* XXXIV (April 1972), 155-172.

Rubinstein, Amnon. "The Occupation: A Sort of Social Revolution," *The New York Times Magazine* (May 6, 1973), pp. 34ff.

Schild, E. O. "On the Meaning of Military Service in Israel," in Curtis, Michael and Chertoff, Mordecai S. (eds.). *Israel: Social Structure and Change.* New Brunswick, New Jersey: Transaction Books, 1973, pp. 419-432.